EVERY
KIND OF
PATCHWORK

EVERY KIND OF PATCHWORK

Text and drawings by
Valerie Campbell-Harding and Michele Walker

EDITED BY KIT PYMAN

SEARCH PRESS LTD

First published 1983
by Search Press Ltd.,
Wellwood, North Farm Road,
Tunbridge Wells, Kent TN2 3DR

Copyright © Search Press Limited 1978, 1983

Reprinted 1984, 1985

Some of the material in this book has been published
in three paperback volumes of the Needle Crafts
series published by Search Press – *Patchwork* (NC4)
and *Patchwork 2* (NC15) by Valerie Campbell-Harding
and *Machine Patchwork* (NC19) by Michel Walker
from which the present volume has been rewritten,
re-illustrated and expanded.

Text and drawings by Valerie Campbell-Harding and
Michel Walker
Editor: Kit Pyman
Photographs by Search Press Studios
Design by Polly Pinder

ISBN (UK) 0 85532 536 4

Page 1: **Snakes and ladders.** *Hand-stitched patchwork
in cottons, spot-quilted at each corner of the square
through thin foam sheeting, and then mounted. Felt
snakes are stuffed and embroidered. Ladders made in
macramé. The counters are single Suffolk puff* (Sheila
Bleasby).

Made and printed in Spain by
A. G. ELKAR, S. Coop.-Autonomía, 71-48012-Bilbao
D. L.: BI-1152-1985

Contents

Introduction

Patchwork is the joining together of pieces of fabric to make a whole. The basic stimulus has always been economy, but patchwork has never been just a question of joining scraps of material but also of conscious artistry in the assembling of the shapes, colours and patterns.

Patchwork has been practised all over the world since the earliest times. In the beginning, skins were patched together to make tents, coverings and armour. One of the oldest pieces of needlework in existence is a patchwork canopy in the Boulak Museum in Cairo. It dates from the ninth century BC, and is made of scraps of gazelle skin dyed and arranged in patterns.

When weaving developed, every thread and length of fabric represented so many hours of painstaking labour that it was necessary to make full use of every fragment, so that for many centuries clothes were simply woven lengths draped over the body. There cannot have been much spare fabric of quality in Europe until the advent of the shaped garment in the Middle Ages, so little work of the early periods has survived.

However, used lengths of fabric were undoubtedly cut up and the least worn areas recycled; for if clothes were discarded before being entirely worn out, then the best parts could be assembled into another article.

A quilt was an excellent form of recycling as it involved three layers of different materials – a patchwork top perhaps, a filling of any yarn or wool or fragments available, and a cheap backing fabric – the whole being stitched together (quilted) into a warm covering.

In Europe patchwork was mainly a cottage craft, born of necessity, though many poor women also worked for their richer neighbours and some made a living from patchwork or quilting. Even among the better off, rich fabrics were too valuable to be discarded, so the remnants were used to make another rich fabric – silks and brocades and velvets being pieced into accessories and furnishings. Many of these pieces were worked by the leisured classes for their own pleasure, often by Applied patchwork methods – the patches being mounted on a backing – because of the different weight of the fabrics. A scrap of silk next to one of velvet will not survive without a common backing.

In Britain, apart from the leisured ladies, patchwork was always associated with poverty and want, and naturally once the urgent need to recycle fabrics had passed so did the craft that sustained it. Now, when patchwork no longer carries the stigma of being a humble thrift craft, new interest has sprung up in the technique which is rapidly developing the status of an art – involving a trained sense of design and skill in treating fabrics with dyes, sprays and stitchery.

In America, the early settlers saw the privations and scarcities of their frontier situation as a challenge rather than a life sentence, and developed the art of patchwork far beyond the simple level obtaining in Britain. They evolved the block pattern, worked by the seamed method (which is much quicker than the English oversewn method), and this enabled them to manage the large volume of fabric involved in making the essential quilts by breaking it down into squares or 'blocks' which could be assembled separately and then 'set' together and stitched into quilts. They also invented social occasions which met their need for company, as well as their need for help in stitching these large areas together, by holding 'Quilting Bees' when the neighbours would arrive with their needles for a day of stitching, friendly gossip and refreshment of body and soul.

It is surprising how many different kinds of patchwork there are; we have gathered examples for this book of all the kinds in general use today and perhaps they will inspire you to try a new way of working (see Glossary on page 111). In the past different methods may have arisen because of the availability of certain kinds of fabric, or in answer to some special need of the times. They all present a fascinating challenge to the needle-woman, for the uses of patchwork are legion.

Oversewn patchwork is the traditional 'English' or mosaic patchwork. Pieces of fabric are cut to shape, tacked over paper templates and the resulting 'patches' are then joined together by hand with oversewing. This is one of the most economical forms of patchwork, as it is possible to make use of even the tiniest scrap of fabric.

In *Applied patchwork* the pieces (or perhaps motifs) are applied to a background. In Crazy and Random patchwork the background is completely covered, and the joins are embellished with stitchery. Swing-stitch patchwork, a modern version, comes under this heading too.

Seamed patchwork differs from oversewn patchwork, for it is based on the dress-making technique of joining the pieces on the wrong side along the seam allowance. American block patchwork comes under this heading, as does

6

Strip patchwork and Seminole – a form of strip patchwork adapted for use on clothes by the Seminole Indians.

Stuffed patchwork is also a dress-making method worked on the machine, and consists of double layers of patches which are filled with wadding, then joined in different ways.

Folded and gathered patchwork is quite different again, as the scraps are folded and pleated and drawn up into shapes before being joined or applied. These techniques include textural effects such as Cathedral Window, Suffolk Puffs and Folded Stars.

Quilting is not typical of patchwork in general – not all quilts are patched, and not all patchwork is quilted – for patchwork and quilting are two separate crafts which are sometimes combined. Block patchwork is nearly always quilted, oversewn patchwork rarely, and folded patchwork never. However the section in this book on quilting applies mainly to Block patchwork and the larger pieces, which may be lightly quilted or tufted. Ideas are offered for various kinds of quilting.

Fabrics for patchwork are often a motley collection. Fabrics in different colours and patterns can be unified by simple dyeing with a commerical dye. Dyeing requires enough pieces of a suitable weight of assorted fabrics for one article. Put them all together in a dyebath of a chosen colour. They will come out all sorts of different shades and tones of that colour, and together can make interesting colour schemes.

A final thought. Artists sign their pictures, but nearly all the needlework that has survived is anonymous. If you spend thought, time and skill on a beautiful piece of work, why not complete it with your signature and the date?

Suffolk puff pram cover. *See pages 96–7.*

Oversewn patchwork

This style of patchwork is also known as 'mosaic' or 'traditional English' patchwork. Fabric pieces are folded and tacked over paper templates, and when enough of these patches have been constructed they are oversewn together on the wrong side. The papers can be taken out when the work is finished.

The whole art of oversewn patchwork is the accuracy with which the paper patterns are cut, and the neatness with which they are covered and joined. Oversewn patchwork has often been used for large quilts and coverlets, but it is particularly suitable for small items as even the tiniest scrap of fabric can be used.

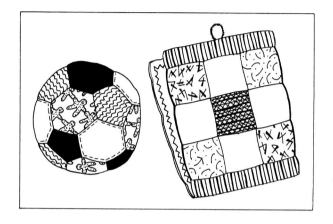

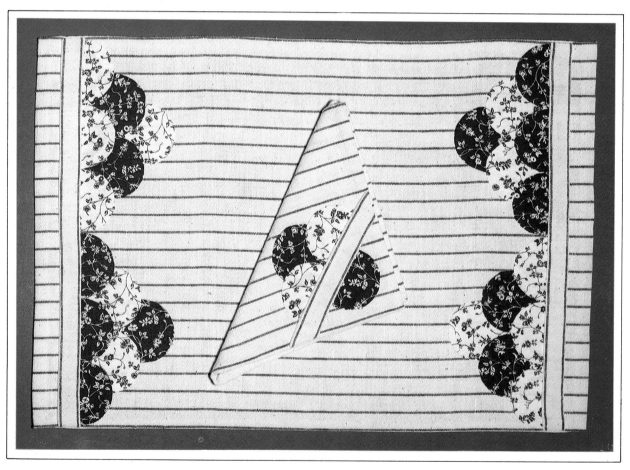

Table Mat and Napkin. *Clamshell patchwork applied to a denim fabric. The hemming is taken through all layers of fabric, and the raw edges are covered with a strip of denim (Pamela Watts).*

Opposite: **Tablecloth.** *Worked in soft cottons using a 1in (25mm) hexagonal template (Brenda Showler).*

8

Materials and equipment

Fabrics

The best fabrics to use are those which have a firm weave, are not too thick and crease well. Cotton is used most often and is probably the most satisfactory. You can also use linen, silk, wool, cotton-and-wool mixtures, corduroy and velvet. Man-made fabrics, except the stretch ones, are less satisfactory as they can pucker and fray too much. If you want to make very small patches, use fine fabrics; thicker fabrics are better for covering large shapes.

Washable fabrics should be washed before being made into patches. Some will shrink more than others, which might cause parts of the finished work to pucker.

Keep the same weight and type of fabric throughout the piece of work. If two patches of different weights are sewn together the heavier one will cause the finer one to tear; also it will be impossible to keep the patches the same size because the one covered with finer fabric will be slightly smaller.

Scissors

You need two pairs – sharp medium-sized scissors for the fabric, and an old pair to cut the paper.

Pins

These should be fine, so that they do not mark the fabric – 'lills' or 'lillikins' are short and do not get in the way.

Thread

Use fine sewing thread; cotton thread will sew most fabrics. Try to match the colour of the thread to the fabric so that it shows less. If you are sewing a dark patch to a light one, use a dark thread.

Needles

Use fine needles – size 9 and 10 are the best – in Sharps and Betweens.

Thimble

A thimble is a help to accurate sewing.

Paper for design

An arithmetic book is useful for planning the designs and the colours can be filled in with a felt pen. Graph paper can be used for designs based on squares, and isometric paper – which is divided into triangles – is used for planning designs that include hexagons, triangles and diamonds.

Board

It is a good idea to have an insulating board, or one made of thick card or cork, on which to pin the patches when planning the design. Pin the completed patches in place too, so that you do not mix them up.

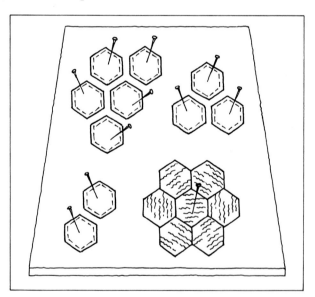

Opposite: **Heart-shaped pincushion.** *Made in cottons with a ⅜in (10mm) hexagon, stuffed with kapok, and mounted on a cardboard base (Brenda Showler).*

Needlecase. *Worked in cotton in hexagons and diamonds, with a Velcro fastening (Brenda Showler).*

10

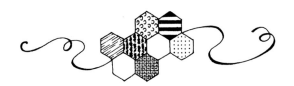

Templates

These are the master shapes from which the paper and fabric patterns are cut. They must be absolutely accurate. Commercial templates – which are available in all sizes and shapes – are made of thin metal and are usually sold in pairs, a solid template the exact size of the patch required, and a 'window' template which is the same shape with a ¼in (6mm) allowance all round for the fabric. The window is made of transparent material, so that the pattern on the fabric can be seen through it and the appropriate section chosen.

Home-made templates can be made from card, but as they do not last very long they are only useful for special projects. If many patterns are going to be cut from them, it is a good idea to make several templates at the beginning.

Even the simplest shape, such as a square, can be divided and rearranged to form an endless number of patterns, as you can see from the patterns opposite.

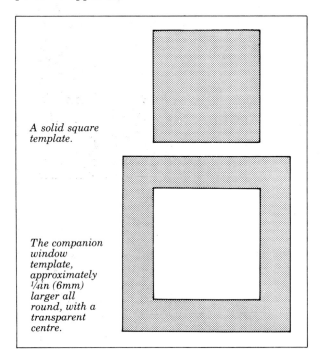

A solid square template.

The companion window template, approximately ¼in (6mm) larger all round, with a transparent centre.

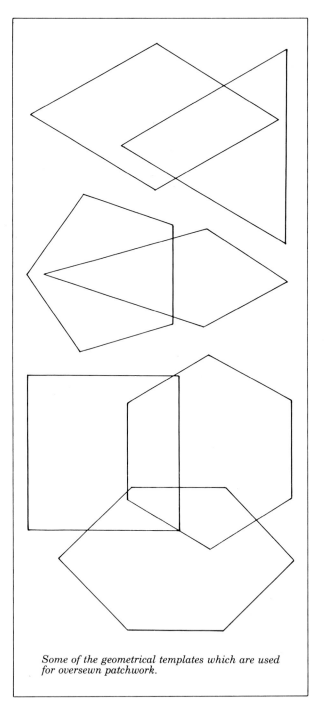

Some of the geometrical templates which are used for oversewn patchwork.

Opposite page: **Patterns using squares.** *Some of the squares have been divided in half to make triangles. They can also be divided to make strips and rectangles.*

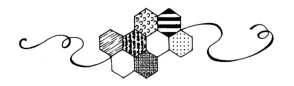

Cutting the patterns

Cut enough paper and fabric patterns for the first section of your design, and then when they are made into patches they can be arranged on your board so that you can see the effect before stitching them together.

Paper patterns

These should be cut from paper or thin card – stiff enough for the edge to be felt through the fold of the fabric. Magazine covers, greetings cards, postcards or thick writing paper are appropriate to different fabrics. Large patches often need thicker paper than small ones, but not so stiff that the paper will not fold with the fabric as the work proceeds.

Cutting out

Paper patterns must be cut very accurately. There are two ways of doing this:–
1. Hold the piece of paper and the template firmly together in one hand so they do not slip, and then cut the paper with the blades of the scissors pressed up against the side of the template. Try to make only one cut for each side of the template. You can cut two paper patterns at once but no more.
2. Lay out the template on the paper on a board and cut it out with a craft knife, pressing the knife against the side of the template.

Fabric patterns

Ideally, the grain of each patch should lie in the same direction – this will make the work crisper and flatter and it will wear better – but this is not always possible if the design suggests otherwise, i.e. when stripes radiate out from a central point.

For a first piece of work, use a fine firm cotton. It is helpful if it has a one-way pattern or stripe that follows the direction of the grain and makes it easier to see.

Cutting out

Use the larger window template to cut the fabric pattern, as it allows adequate turnings and shows what the finished patch will look like. There are two methods of cutting out fabric patterns:–
1. Hold the template and fabric firmly together and cut round the edges close to the template.
2. Draw round the template with a dressmakers' pencil and then cut out.

Cutting a paper pattern.

Window template laid on the fabric to show the effect of the finished patch.

Opposite: **Cotton cushion.** *A traditional design in floral patterned cottons in shades of brown and cream* (Anne West).

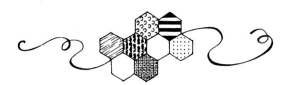

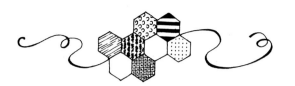

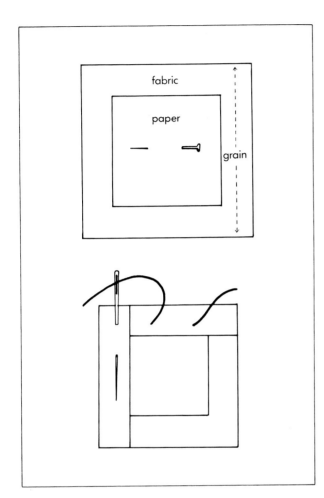

Making the patches

The most usual way is as follows:

Tacking

Lay the paper pattern in the centre of the fabric patch, on the reverse side. Pin the two together through the centre. Fold one edge of fabric over the paper and take a large stitch through all three layers. (If the fabric is likely to mark, tack through the turning and the paper only.)

Fold the second side of fabric over the paper and take a stitch through the fold; then take another stitch through the centre of the side – with very small patches one stitch will do instead of two. Continue round all the sides, taking an extra stitch in the first side, and leave a short length of thread hanging free.

The beginning of the thread can be knotted if you wish but if you are making a large piece of work it will be much easier to take the tacking threads out at the end if there are no knots. The papers are left in the work until it is finished in order to keep it crisp and fresh.

The paper pattern can be replaced with one of vilene, felt, thin foam or another material, depending on the result you require. Since these are quite difficult to handle they are best forgotten until some experience is gained with the paper patterns. Patterns of felt and vilene are left in when the work is finished to add body.

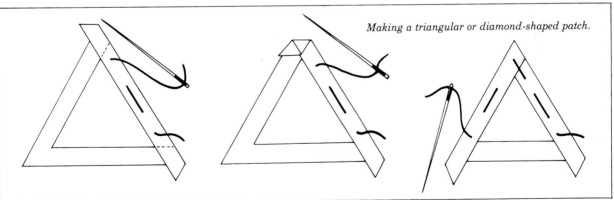

Making a triangular or diamond-shaped patch.

Sewing

Patches are usually joined together by holding two patches together with the right sides of the fabric facing each other and the papers on the outside, and oversewing along the edge. Start the sewing about ¼in (6mm) in from the corner, work back to the corner, then sew forwards to the next corner. Finish off by working back again for ¼in (6mm). Make neat stitches by taking only a small

Opposite: **Cushion pad.** *Designed to fit a cane-seated chair, this cushion is made of a mixture of plain and flowered cottons with a 2in (5cm) diamond template. Padded with terylene wadding and piped in a plain colour (Frances Collins).*

amount of fabric each time and not sewing through the paper. With fine fabrics, sixteen stitches to 1in (25mm) will be about right.

When the seam is finished and the patches are opened out the stitches will show on the right side and therefore must be even. You can sometimes seam together several patches with the same thread.

Pressing

When the patches have all been sewn together, remove the tacking threads. Then press the work on the wrong side and carefully take out the papers. Sometimes they can be used again.

Lining

Most patchwork should be lined to add body and hide the raw edges (it is unnecessary to line patchwork intended for cushions). Cut a piece of backing the same size as the top, but including the seam allowances. Place the right sides together and smooth them flat. Pin, then tack around the three edges and sew together. Turn to the right side and hem-stitch the remaining edge by hand. For extra weight and warmth the work can be interlined with flannel or wadding, and the three layers can be quilted or knotted together.

Edges

1. The lining can be machined with the right sides inside, and then turned right side out.

Detail of tablecloth shown on page 9.

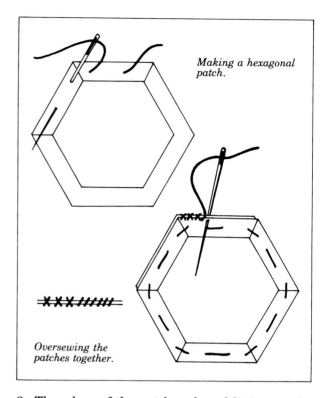

Making a hexagonal patch.

Oversewing the patches together.

2. The edges of the patchwork and lining can be tacked together and bound with a strip of fabric.
3. Another method is to fold the edges of the patchwork and lining to the inside and then stitch through all the layers close to the edge, either by machine or with a running stitch. Whichever method you use, choose it because it is appropriate to the article you are making.

Design

Colour and tone

These are very important in patchwork, with tone (which means how light or dark the colour is) being the most important. A patch that is the wrong colour is not nearly so noticeable as one that is too light or too dark. The importance of tone is shown by the three-dimensional effects obtained when dark, medium and light patches are sewn together in various ways. Closely related colours make a pleasant muted scheme whereas contrasting colours are lively. For a first piece of work you can choose three related colours, such as blue, green and turquoise, with one of the colours fairly dark and one fairly pale. If the tones are too alike the pattern will be lost. Try to vary the proportions of the three colours and do not use equal quantities of any of them.

Collect as many fabrics as you can so that you have a piece of the right colour in your design.

Stripes

Striped fabrics have immense possibilities in patchwork and a single piece of striped fabric can, with careful cutting and planning, be used to make a complete article. A plain fabric can be combined with a striped one to emphasize the pattern.

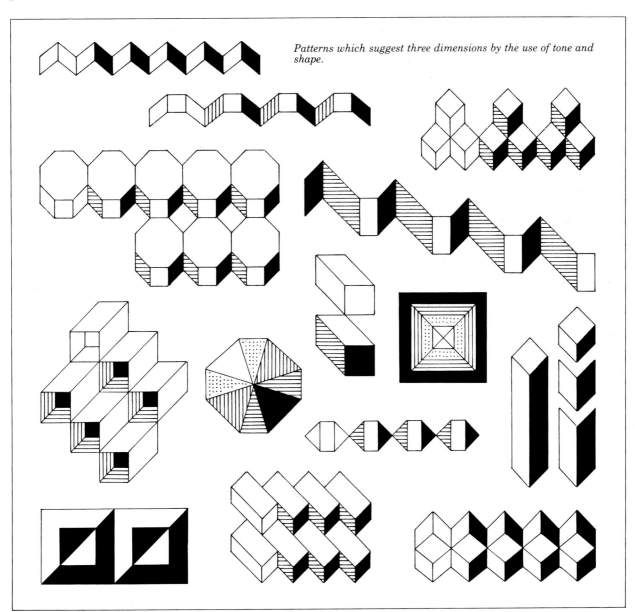

Patterns which suggest three dimensions by the use of tone and shape.

Geometrical patterns

A vast range of patterns can be made by using bought templates in geometrical shapes. It is almost impossible for two people to produce the same design, even if they use the same shapes and fabrics. The easiest shape to make in patchwork is the hexagon, but the long hexagon has more possibilities for pattern-making, and combines well with other shapes. The square is extremely useful for it can be sub-divided into triangles, rectangles, stripes and many more. The diamond is difficult to make because of the sharp point. Leave it until more experience is gained.

Geometrical shapes can be put together in long strips and then sewn together along the length. One strip could be of small squares, the next of triangles, the next of larger squares, and so on. This could be built up to make a complete cushion cover, skirt, or window blind. For a bed-cover, it would probably be more satisfactory to work outwards from a central square or rectangle.

Try to mix different shapes in your design to add variety. Many pieces of work can have a border around them or along one edge. The border colours can be paler or darker than the main part and the shapes can be larger or altogether different.

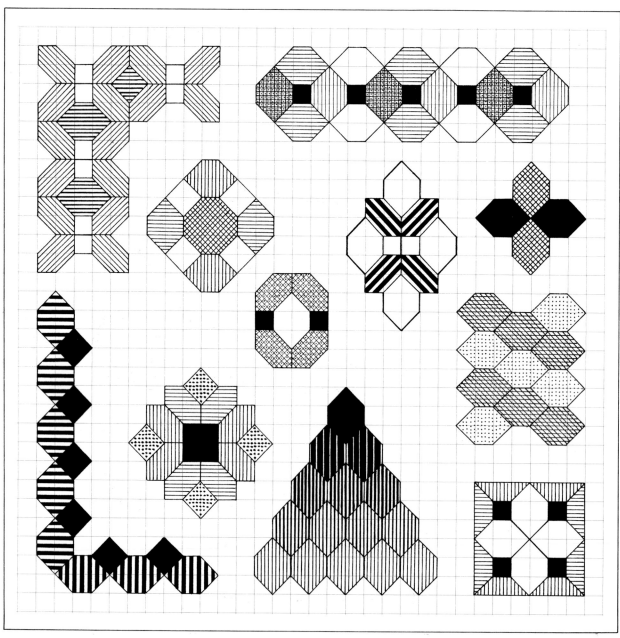

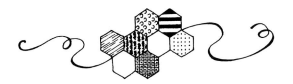

Right: *Interlaced octagon pattern. The shapes have been put together using the basic shapes — triangles, squares and octagons — shown at the top left-hand corner of the diagram.*

Opposite: *Patterns using long hexagons combined with squares, octagons and half-hexagons, drawn on squared paper.*

Below: **Satin cushion.** *Designed to be used in a modern setting of black leather and chrome, this traditional pattern has been made with unusual fabric — black, white and striped satin, using a hexagonal template (Helen Clarke).*

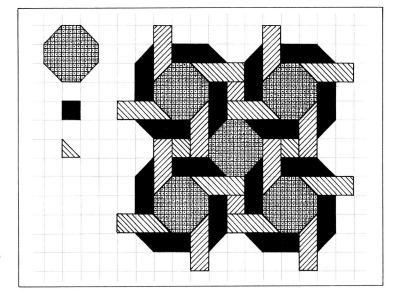

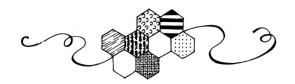

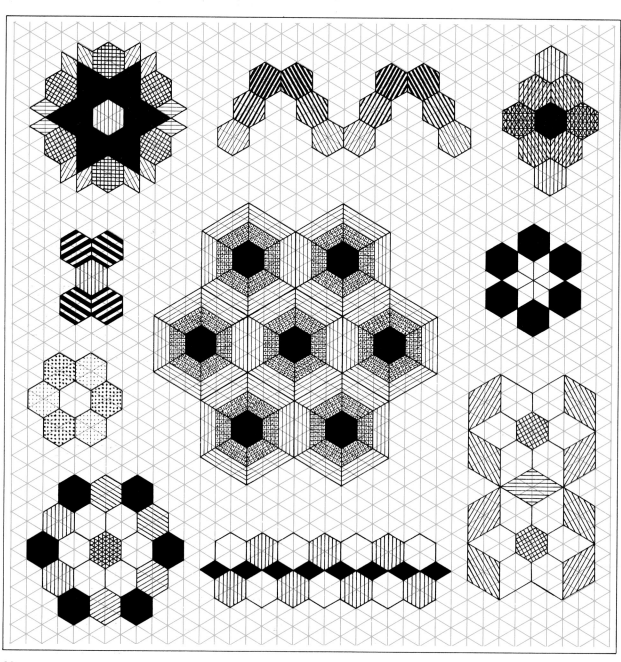

Borders

Many kinds of patchwork make interesting borders which can be pieced or applied to the main fabric. A patchwork border will extend the area round a square of printed fabric or a piece of embroidery, and will also form a decorative frame. Borders can be placed on the edges of curtains, blinds or tablecloths, around the bottom of jackets or skirts, along yokes, and round cuffs and down the front of tops and dresses.

Most quilts, whatever the pattern, look better with a border. Medallion quilts are almost all border, with small central area which is often of printed fabric. Some furnishing fabrics with a large motif would make an ideal centrepiece, surrounded with successive borders. It is often a good idea to combine the same pattern on a different scale in one piece of work: for example to make a border of small diamonds, then one of squares, then one of larger diamonds, and join them all together. The smaller shapes should be placed towards the middle of the article.

Corners

These need careful planning. Some patterns will not turn a corner successfully, and the space must therefore be filled with a plain shape such as a square, or a sub-divided square. If you are not sure how well a pattern will turn a corner, hold a small flat mirror at right angles to the pattern and adjust it until you can see the result you want.

Other sources of patterns

Mosaics, stained-glass windows, tiled floors and other architectural details can all suggest patchwork patterns. Other crafts such as beadwork from Africa or North America, rugs, and woven cane chair seats all have patterns which might be adapted. Nature is also a rich source of inspiration, and close-up photographs of many plants, shells, insect wings or leaves reveal intricate patterns that are not at first easily seen.

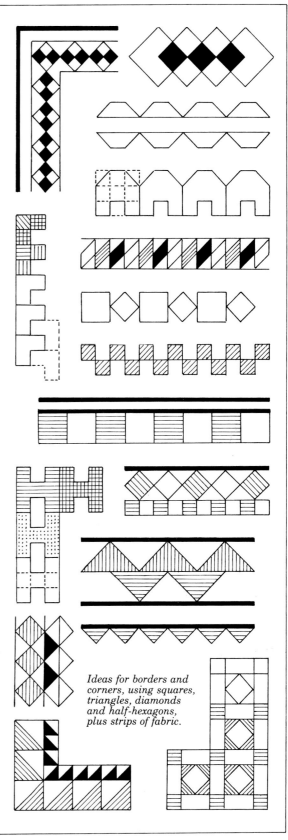

Ideas for borders and corners, using squares, triangles, diamonds and half-hexagons, plus strips of fabric.

Opposite: Patterns using hexagons, half-hexagons, pentagons and diamonds, drawn on isometric paper.

Compass star quilt

A large star design pieced into a background consisting mostly of hexagons, surrounded with a formal border of hexagons, diamonds and strips. The design is shown below, drawn out on isometric paper. Although the pieces appear to fit perfectly, remember that when large patches are allied with much smaller ones, allowance must be made for the extra width taken up by the thickness of fabric where the small patches join. One way of ensuring this is to make the smaller paper patches fractionally smaller than the design would indicate. The other way is to make up the patches, match them to the larger one and then trim the paper patch of the larger one to fit the assembled small ones.

Although the background is white it shows great variety of tone and texture, because it is made of old evening shirts with their woven and raised patterns, which give interest to the surface of the patchwork. (*Anne Dyer*)

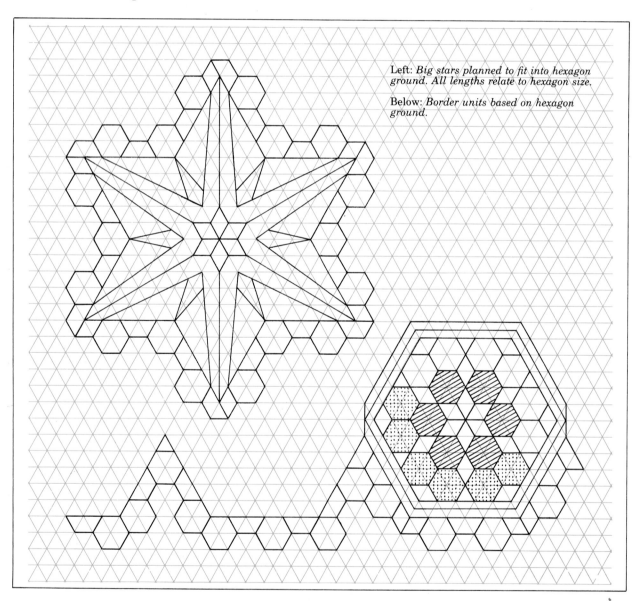

Left: *Big stars planned to fit into hexagon ground. All lengths relate to hexagon size.*

Below: *Border units based on hexagon ground.*

Opposite: **Quilt.** *Compass star shapes in a background of hexagons* (Anne Dyer).

Clamshell patchwork

This method is also known as 'Shell' or 'Fish-scale' patchwork from the shape of the templates. These are made in pairs, one in solid metal and one slightly larger window template. It is better to buy these than to make them, since constructing them accurately is difficult. A paper and patch method is used to make the shapes, which are built up in overlapping rows to form a fabric, each row being stitched to the previous one. Choose soft but firmly woven fabrics, and use matching thread.

Design ideas

As Clamshell patchwork generally produces an overall design of the same shapes, variety is best achieved by changes of colour, pattern and texture. The curved lines and unified pattern are ideal for small items, and small areas make a good applied decoration for clothes and household linen. Pin out the patches on your board when planning the design.

Preparation

Make a paper patch as follows: place the solid template on thin card, draw around it with a sharp pencil and cut on this line.

Make a number of fabric patches as follows: place the window template on the straight grain of the fabric, hold the two together or draw around with a soft pencil, and cut around the shape.

Sewing

Pin the paper shape in the centre of the *right side* of a fabric patch. Turn them over, and with the *wrong side* of the fabric uppermost tack down the semi-circular edge, making small pleated folds, following exactly the curve of the paper.

Make sure the fabric is not sewn to the paper patterns. Unpin the paper and use it for the next patch. Use a new paper shape when the old one becomes worn. Make the required number of patches.

To assemble the patches, pin the first row on a board in a straight line, right side up, with the sides of each patch just touching. Pin the second row in place, overlapping the first by ¼in (6mm) and covering the raw edges. Hem each row to the next along the convex edge.

When two areas of scales are placed in opposite directions, the central patches can be circular, as shown in the cushion illustrated.

Finishing

Clamshell patchwork should be lined. The raw edges of the last row can be concealed in a seam where applicable, or covered with a strip of fabric. See the table mat and napkin, designed by Pamela Watts, on page 8.

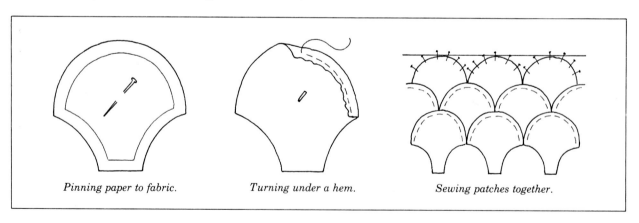

Pinning paper to fabric.   *Turning under a hem.*   *Sewing patches together.*

Opposite: **Clamshell patchwork cushion.** *An overall pattern of Clamshell patchwork. The two opposing rows of scales are joined with circular patches in the centre (Pamela Watts).*

Applied patchwork

Most types of patchwork can be made up and then applied to a plain piece of fabric. This is quicker than making a whole patchwork article, and the plain areas show up the pattern. Applied patchwork can be placed centrally, arranged as separate motifs as in the examples shown, or used as a border. In some varieties of patchwork, pieces are laid on a background and sewn in place – generally the patches cover the whole area and the background fabric is not visible – and sometimes the joins are covered with decorative stitchery.

Crazy patchwork, Random patchwork and Swingstitch patchwork are all different ways of

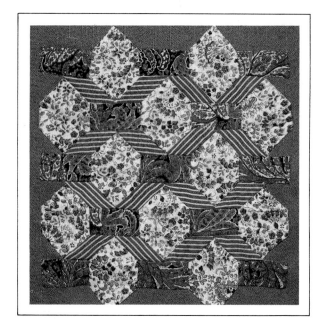

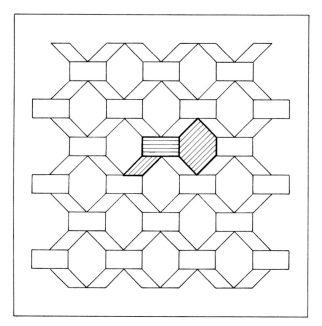

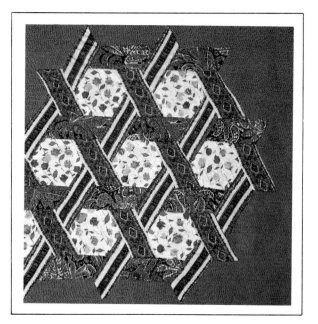

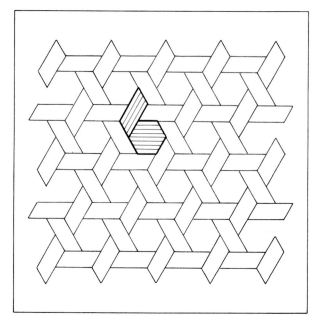

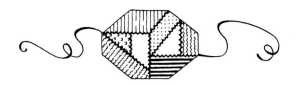

arranging patches on a backing. One type of Log Cabin patchwork is worked on a background, the strips being stitched to the backing fabric in a certain order. The other type of Log Cabin patchwork is seamed – which is quicker, though not so suitable for delicate fabrics – and will be found on pages 57–8.

The backing fabric for these applied patchwork techniques is usually calico or plain cotton. A newcomer to these backings is iron-on vilene, where the patches can be ironed in place and the joins covered with stitchery.

Opposite and below: **Applied patchwork.** *These patchwork motifs were applied to a plain fabric and made into a hanging. The designs were taken from windows in various chateaux in the Loire district in France.*

The sketches were drawn out on squared paper, and master templates were cut from heavy sandpaper. The patchwork was made up by the oversewn method, and the completed designs applied to the background fabric with slip stitch (Pat Salmon).

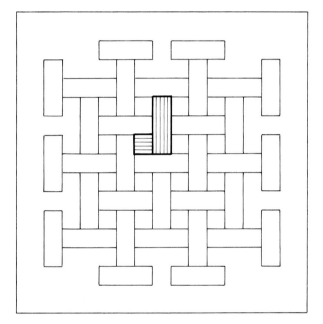

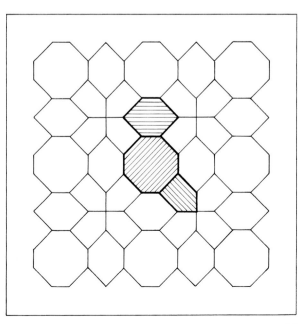

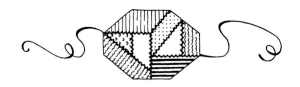

Applying motifs and borders

When pieces and strips of patchwork are to be applied to an area of plain fabric, keep the overall shape simple and try to avoid awkward corners and sharp points, as these are often difficult to deal with.

Design ideas

Stars or rosettes made up of triangles, diamonds or hexagons can be applied to a square of fabric and used for a bag or cushion, to make the top of a box or as a centrepiece for a quilt. Patchwork borders can be applied all round.

Flower and leaf shapes can be built up from triangles and squares, and abstract patterns from

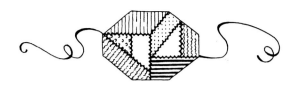

a combination of diamonds, octagons and squares. Curved shapes are especially suitable for applied patchwork, as it is easier to apply curves than to piece them. Strips of patchwork can be applied across the yoke or around the sleeve of ready-made clothes to add colour and individuality.

Preparation

Make up the patchwork and press it on the wrong side. If the paper and patch (oversewn) method is used the edges will be already folded, but the papers should be taken out and the turnings pressed again to make them lie flat. Thicker fabrics, and felt and leather, can be left with a raw edge, but otherwise a ¼in (6mm) hem is turned under if required.

Sewing

The patchwork can be applied by hand or by machine. Sew the folded edge to the plain fabric with hem stitch, slip stitch or stab stitch – slip stitch being the least visible. Alternatively a small running stitch can be worked close to the edge. Raw edges can be covered with herringbone stitch, or swing-stitched by machine.

Finishing

Press carefully on the right side over a thick towel.

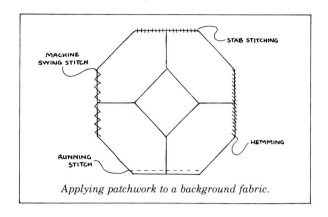

Applying patchwork to a background fabric.

Opposite: **Patchwork box.** *The box was built upon a cardboard roll. The applied shapes are slightly raised, and consist of five equilateral triangles (with the tips cut off) arranged in a circle, worked by the oversewn method and joined with decorative stitchery. Four of these shapes are placed around the box on the outside, and the fifth is on the lid. A pentagon ball makes the knob (Daisy Hughes).*

Above: **Curtain edge.** *A patchwork border which was pieced, and applied to a cotton curtain, which was then quilted (Valerie Campbell-Harding).*

31

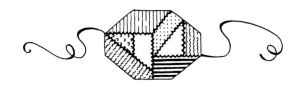

Swing-stitch patchwork

Patches made of leather or felt or plastic can be cut leaving no seam allowance, placed edge to edge on the backing fabric with corners matching, and swing-stitched on the right side.

Finer fabrics, or those which fray, should be backed with iron-on vilene before the swing-stitching. Cut out the piece of vilene, lay the patches in place right way up, starting at one edge, and when a row is in position iron them in place so that they are firmly held. Do not allow the iron to go over the edge of the fabric or the base will become sticky. Place a second row in position and iron it down. Continue until a large area is covered with patches, and then swing-stitch them around each piece on the right side.

Below: **Table mat.** *Patches applied to a vilene backing and swing-stitched in place. The mat is baked with towelling (Valerie Campbell-Harding).*

Opposite: **Ludo.** *Hand stitched patchwork in cottons form the background, and the corner motifs of baskets and flowers were applied by machine. The patchwork is spot quilted to a thin foam sheeting and backed with cotton. The counters are single Suffolk Puffs (Sheila Bleasby).*

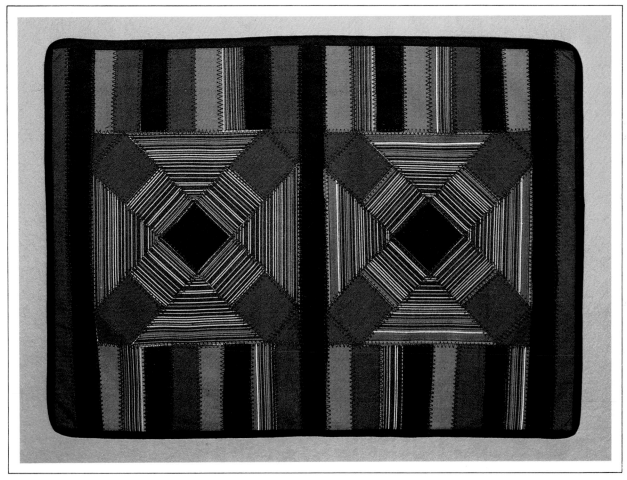

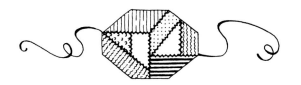

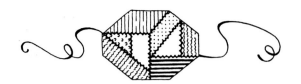

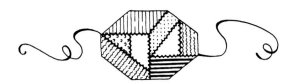

Ideas for applied motifs.

Right: *The Tumbling Blocks pattern uses a diamond template, and the three-dimensional effect is achieved by the use of tone – an arrangement of dark, medium and light colours in a regular pattern.*

Opposite: **Applied patchwork cushion.** *The patches have been applied to a vilene background with machine zig-zag. The pattern, which is known as 'Tumbling Blocks', gives a three-dimensional effect* (Valerie Campbell-Harding).

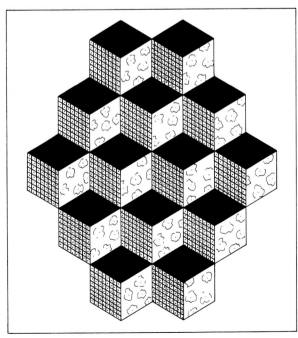

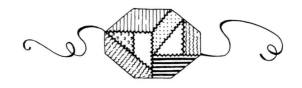

Random patchwork

Random patchwork consists of geometric shapes, usually squares and rectangles, of varying sizes, which are fitted together more or less haphazardly and sewn to a backing fabric.

Design ideas

As this form of patchwork is made from many different shapes and sizes the design possibilities are more limited than with other forms of patchwork. The size of the pieces can be graded from small to large in one article, or the pieces can be put together to form squares or triangles or wide strips which are then sewn together with a ¼in (6mm) seam to make a more controlled design.

Traditional technique with plain backing

Preparation

Cut out a number of fabric patches. Cut a piece of cotton or calico slightly larger than is needed, and mark the area to be covered with a hard pencil. Then starting from one corner, lay the shapes on the calico overlapping the raw edges by about ¼in (6mm). Pin carefully.

Sewing

Sew around the overlapping edges with running stitch. Add more pieces, pin and sew. Continue until the whole area is covered.

Left: **Waistcoat.** *Random patchwork in blue and cream, machine-quilted after assembly* (Jane Lemon).

Opposite: **Child's waistcoat.** *Random patchwork in related colours, quilted by hand after assembly* (Valerie Campbell-Harding).

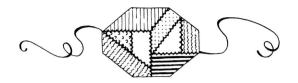

Modern technique with padded backing

This makes a more solid fabric, and is stitched by machine. It can be done by hand but the results are not so satisfactory.

Preparation

Cut the fabric pieces together with thin wadding, and treat as one. Pin the pieces to the backing, touching each other.

Sewing

Work close machine zig-zag all around the edge of each padded piece. Place a few more pieces-plus-wadding next to the stitched ones, pin and sew. Continue until the whole area is covered.

Finishing

Two methods. The traditional technique adds a lining when the article is made up. The modern technique quilts the patchwork and does not require lining.

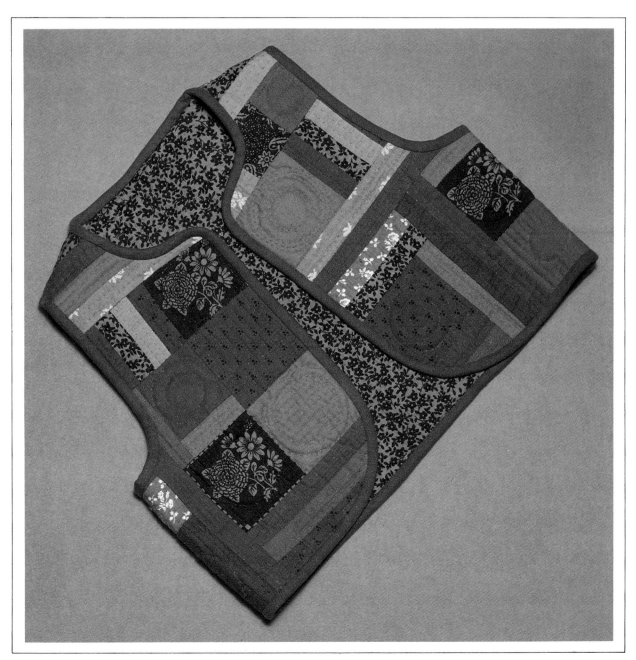

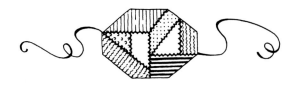

Crazy patchwork

Crazy patchwork uses scraps of fabric of any shape or size, which are stitched to a backing fabric, usually cotton or calico. Traditionally, feather stitching or herringbone stitch covered the raw edges; today machine zig-zag or satin stitch can be used instead. The surface stitching should be worked in one-colour thread over the whole piece to unify it.

Most types of fabric are suitable, including silks, wools, velvet and leather – but it is best to keep to one type of fabric in one article.

Design ideas

In Crazy patchwork these will depend upon the scraps available. As in the geometrical Random patchwork, you could grade the sizes of the scraps, or join some together into larger units. The problem has been solved in the garment opposite with the use of colour and pattern – two printed fabrics and two plain ones in related colours.

Preparation

Cut the scraps to a convenient size and trim any frayed edges. Cut out a piece of backing fabric a little larger than the finished size, and mark around the shape with a pencil. Starting from one corner, lay the shapes on the backing, either overlapping the edges or turning under a hem where it covers the previous patch.

Sewing

Sew each patch on in turn. Continue until the whole area is covered. Finally, work an embroidery stitch over all the joins.

Finishing

Garments will have to be lined to cover the stitchery, but other items, such as cushion covers, need not be lined.

Crazy patchwork is not usually quilted.

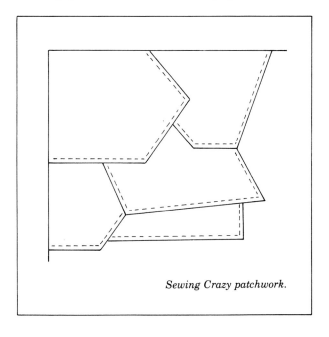

Sewing Crazy patchwork.

Opposite: **Child's anorak.** *The Crazy patchwork for this anorak was worked on a commercial pattern. The paper pattern was cut out of muslin, and the first patch was attached to one corner of the foundation fabric with running stitches. A hem was folded down on a second patch, where it covered the first, and this patch was secured through all layers. When all the foundation fabric was covered, the joins were decorated with herringbone stitch, buttonhole and feather stitch. Finally, the garment was made up, and lined (Margaret Cheetham).*

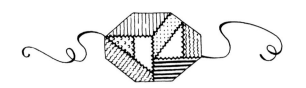

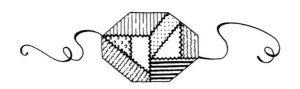

Log Cabin patchwork – applied

(For the seamed method see page 57)

This is a quick and adaptable form of patchwork, easy to make, and one which does not require templates. Strips of fabric are applied to a background fabric to form a square, and then a number of squares are joined together to make a larger area.

Fabric

In general, the same weight of fabric should be used throughout – cotton with cotton, wool with wool etc. Choose a weight suitable for your purpose. However, as this kind of patchwork is backed, it is possible to vary the materials where laundering is not a problem, for example the bag on page 43 combines fabric and snake-skin.

Plain and printed fabrics are often combined, or ribbon or tape, or any fabric in strip form.

Design

Traditionally, the squares were made up with half the strips in light tones and half in dark – it was felt that a strong contrast was required to emphasize the pattern. However, it is also possible to work in a single colour or fabric, such as calico or shot silk, which will show up the design by shadows or the play of light on silk.

Size

The size of the squares can vary. A cushion, for example, might consist of a single square, or four or more. Squares can always be enlarged with the addition of a few more strips. A square for a quilt could be as large as 12in (30cm).

Pattern

If you wish to work out the amount of fabric needed, you can draw a diagram of one square on graph paper which will give you the width and length of each strip and the size of the central square. However, most people do not bother with a pattern but fit the strips in place and cut them as required.

Cutting out

Cut a piece of backing fabric (calico, cotton or old sheeting will do) the size of the finished square, with a seam allowance all round. Cut out the central square of fabric.

Press the main fabrics, lay them face down on a flat surface and mark long strips with pencil and ruler, allowing a ¼in (6mm) seam allowance each side. Cut these out along the grain – do not tear as this distorts the fabric.

Preparation

Crease the backing square diagonally, or draw a pencil line from each corner to mark the centre. Lay the central square in place and secure with pins or tacking.

There are two methods of applying the strips, depending on the sequence in which they are sewn to the backing.

Method 1

The strips are stitched in place in turn in a clockwise direction, lapping over each other. Cut one strip the length of one side of the central

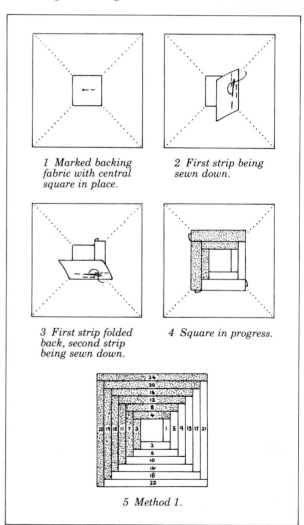

1 Marked backing fabric with central square in place.

2 First strip being sewn down.

3 First strip folded back, second strip being sewn down.

4 Square in progress.

5 Method 1.

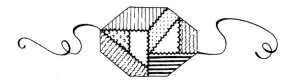

square. Lay it face down on one side of the central square, raw edges level, and sew down the seam line through all three layers by hand or by machine.

Fold this strip back and press. Cut the next strip the length of one side of the square plus the width of the strip already sewn. Lay it in place, face down, and stitch across the seam line. Continue adding strips in a clockwise direction until the square is completed.

When several squares have been made they are seamed together on the reverse side, and the seams are pressed open. A lining or backing may be required to finish the article. The diagram shows a traditional pattern of strips where the light tones are used for the first two sides and the dark tones for the other two. When these completed squares are joined together, another pattern emerges according to the arrangement of the squares. (*For Method 2, see next page.*)

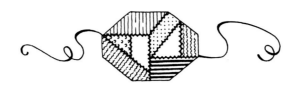

Method 2

This method is sometimes called 'Courthouse Steps', and the strips are applied to the backing in pairs around the central fabric.

The pairs of strips can be of different widths, or wide and narrow alternately, or in light and dark tones, or two dark and two light, or in different colours. The central piece of fabric can be square or rectangular or just a strip, and it need not be in the centre – it can be off-centre or in one corner.

Cut a backing square the required size, the central piece of fabric and a collection of strips. Pin or tack the centrepiece in position. Cut two strips the same width as the centrepiece and stitch them in place, the same way as Method 1, at the top and bottom. Fold back and press. Cut two strips the same length as the centrepiece plus the width of the two strips already in position, and stitch them down each side. Fold back and press.

Continue in this way until the background is covered.

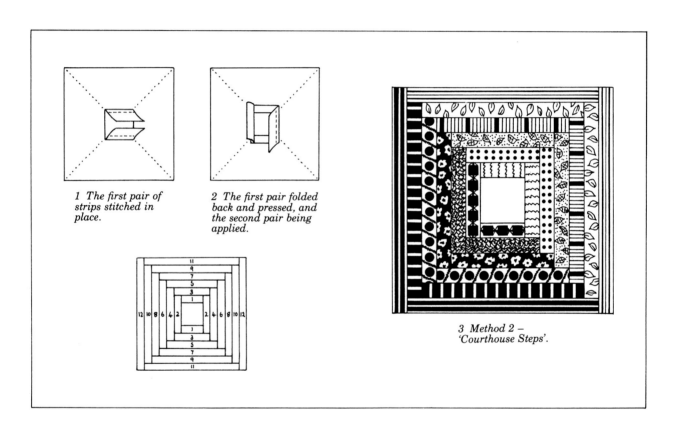

1 The first pair of strips stitched in place.

2 The first pair folded back and pressed, and the second pair being applied.

3 Method 2 – 'Courthouse Steps'.

Previous page: **Applied Log Cabin cushion.** *Four squares of Log Cabin patchwork are fitted together to make this cushion (Valerie Tulloch).*

Opposite: **Applied Log Cabin handbag.** *Two squares of Log Cabin patchwork form the flap of this bag, with an unusual combination of fabrics – flowered cottons and wools and snakeskin (Stephanie Wood).*

Seamed patchwork

Seamed patchwork consists of simple shapes, cut out with a seam allowance and joined together on the reverse side as in dressmaking.

The easiest form of seamed patchwork is Strip patchwork, where strips of different fabrics and widths are stitched together. A more elaborate form is known as 'Seminole' patchwork, where areas of seamed strips are re-cut, re-arranged and sewn together to make elaborate patterns.

Log Cabin is also a form of strip patchwork. This can be made by the Applied method (see pages 38–41); the seamed method is, however, not only quicker but more suitable for large items which are to be quilted.

'Block' patterns were evolved to simplify the making of large articles such as coverlets and quilts. By this means the amount of fabric to be handled could be made up in manageable blocks each about 1ft (30cm) square, consisting of one or several different patchwork patterns, and only when all the blocks were made was the quilt assembled in its entirety.

Templates are used for block patchwork, generally simple geometric shapes with straight sides. Curves can be introduced into these designs, giving a more flowing overall design, but the technique of joining curved seams requires considerable skill.

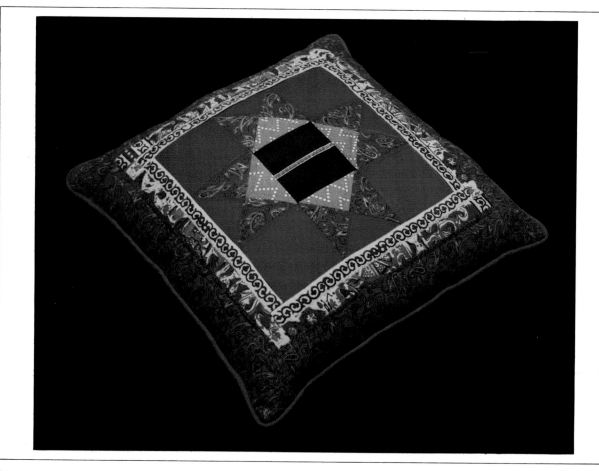

Below and opposite: **Pair of cushions.**
*These two cushions were made from the
same collection of scraps in two different
patterns.*
Left: *The cushion has a central 'Variable
Star' block, with three borders, two
narrow and one wide. It is machine-pieced,
and hand-quilted ¼in (6mm) from the
outline of the star shape. The 'Variable
Star' block pattern is shown on page 61.*
Right: *The 'Grandmother's Fan' block was
machine-pieced, and a border added all
round. Cotton lace was applied to the edge
of the fan. The fan shape is hand-quilted
'in the ditch'.* (June Bowles)

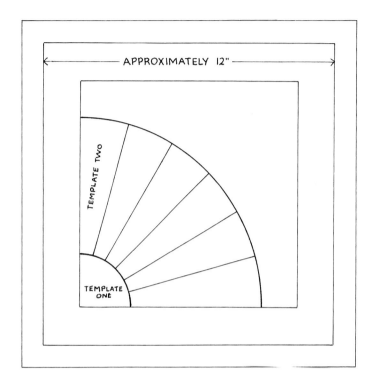

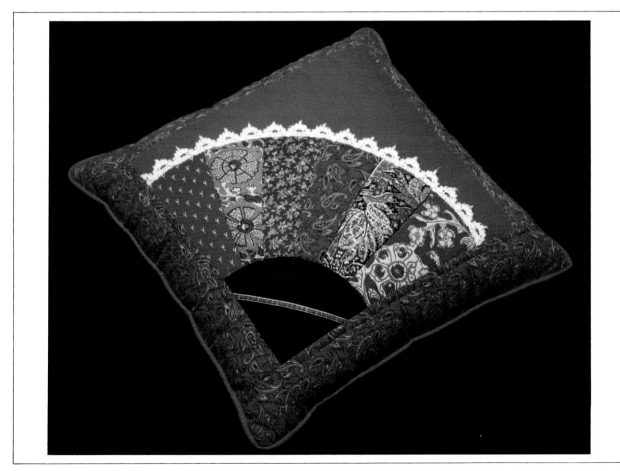

Equipment

Since seamed patchwork, like most other kinds of patchwork, requires very accurate measuring and cutting the best results will be achieved if you invest in a few basic tools.

For designing and making templates

Coloured pencils and felt tip pens; square and triangular graph paper; hard pencil; scissors (for cutting paper); scalpel knife with replaceable blades; spray adhesive; heavyweight card; set-square.

For stitching

A sewing machine that makes a good even running-stitch, and preferably a reverse stitch: a steam iron and pressing cloth; needles; cotton-polyester thread; lace pins; seam ripper; dressmaker's scissors and small scissors for cutting ends; tape measure.

For quilting

Quilting hoop; needles 'betweens' 8–9; thimble; quilting thread and beeswax; coloured pencil; rug thread.

Fabrics

The fabrics for machine patchwork are chosen with the same considerations as those for other kinds of patchwork – design, use and washability. However, where quilts are concerned, three materials are involved – the top fabric, the wadding and the backing.

Top fabric

Cotton dress-weight fabrics are the easiest to use. They are very hard-wearing and give excellent results. They press well and are suitable for all shapes. It is important, if the patchwork is to be washed, that the fabrics are pre-shrunk and fast dyed. (Batiks and Indian cotton fabrics do not seem to retain the dye well.) Today cotton fabrics are often replaced with cotton/polyester mixtures which tend to be springy and crease-resistant. These are much easier to sew by machine than by hand. When they are mixed with cotton fabrics, however, take special care with the ironing of the completed patchwork, as polyesters require a much lower ironing temperature than cottons.

The strength of machine sewing enables a great range of fabrics to be considered for making patchwork. Tweeds, suitings, corduroys, denim and gabardine all have interesting textures and, providing the patches are fairly large and simple, can be used successfully for warm bed quilts, curtains and floor coverings.

Do not mix fabrics of varying weights within a patchwork project as the heavier ones tend to pull and tear the lighter patches. Avoid stretchy fabrics that do not retain the correct size and shape. If the patchwork is to be hand-quilted, choose a soft fabric.

Wadding or filling

If you intend to quilt your patchwork a wadding or filling is sandwiched between the top and the backing. There is a variety available – the washable, synthetic Terylene and Courtelle waddings are very popular, lightweight and easy to use. They come in different weights: the 2oz (60g) is the thinnest and easiest for both hand and machine quilting, the bouncy 4oz (125g) and 8oz (250g) weights are best for knotting or tufting. Cotton wadding, woollen and cotton domettes are heavier than the synthetic waddings but less bulky. They add weight to a quilt but create a flatter effect. They are excellent for machine quilting.

Backing fabric

Cheaper dress-weight cottons are suitable for most patchwork backing. Whether a patchwork is going to be hand-quilted or machine-quilted affects the choice of fabrics. For hand-quilting choose a backing fabric that is soft and easy to pierce with a needle. Sheeting, although the size is ideal, is often so closely woven that quilting is made difficult.

Choosing fabric patterns

Using fabrics together successfully is often more difficult than acquiring the techniques of sewing patchwork together. Combining different patterned fabrics comes with practice, but patchwork designs need contrast to be effective.

A variety of shapes, lights and darks, and different scales of pattern will give more exciting design than a collection of small-scale prints which eliminate the individual shapes and produce a generally bland effect. Have a variety of fabrics in prints and plain colours, combine small, medium and large-scale prints together, and use border patterns to frame a design. Curved patterns often create a sense of movement, while stripes give direction to a design – they are also good for lattice strips.

Choosing colours

Colours change next to each other. What may appear to be a dark patch often seems much lighter beside another fabric.

Generally bright and light colours stand out, while dark and dull colours recede; but if you are not sure of the tonal value look at them with your eyes half-closed to eliminate the pattern.

A scrap quilt is often the most difficult to plan because of the variety of prints. It is then useful either to sort the fabrics into lights and darks, or to supplement them with a quantity of fabric in a single colour. Buying bags of scraps (providing they are good value) or exchanging fabrics with friends can introduce fresh colours and patterns that you may not have considered choosing for yourself. Try and build up your own collection of fabrics – buy them when you see something interesting – colours are much influenced by fashion and are often only available for one season. The quilt below is made from a family scrap bag. See caption next page.

Strip patchwork

Using strips of fabric in patchwork is an economical method which also makes for interesting patterns. A ruler or yardstick is a useful template and is always accurate.

Design ideas

Long strips of fabric can be sewn together, then cut up across the seams and joined to other shapes, or to each other with the strips going in different directions.

Geometric shapes such as triangles can be sewn together in long strips, and then joined to plain fabric or to strips of other shapes. Strips can also be used to frame a central geometric shape, and can become wider at the outer edge. This looks particularly effective on cushions.

Preparation

Lay the ruler on the back of the fabric along the grain and draw along the edge with a hard pencil or dressmakers' pencil. Include a ¼in (6mm) seam allowance in the width of the strip. Draw a number of strips of different widths and cut them out accurately. Lay two together and pin at intervals along one edge.

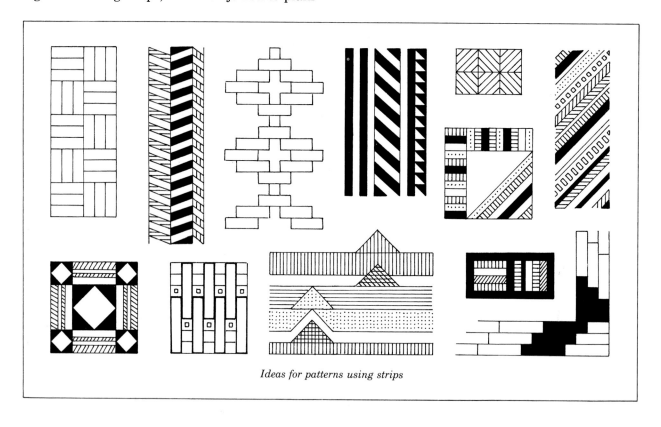

Ideas for patterns using strips

Previous page: **Hotpotch quilt.** *This quilt is made from sentimental scraps of cotton backed with an old flannelette sheet. The lattice strips are cut from old shirts, and the edges are bound with flowered fabric. This is an example of a traditional simple 'block' pattern, called the 'Churn Dash' block. Twenty-five blocks have been joined together to make a quilt. The patchwork is done on the machine, the quilting is done by hand but is minimal to allow the fabric pattern full emphasis* (Phyllis Harris).

Opposite: **Strip patchwork bag.** *Plain and flowered fabrics joined in strips to make a bag, quilted by machine along the seam lines* (Valerie Campbell-Harding).

Sewing

The best method is to machine-stitch ¼in (6mm) from one edge, using the edge of the presser foot as a guide.

Press the seam to one side. Join all your strips together in pairs, and then join all the pairs together.

Finishing

The patchwork must be lined or backed, so that the edges do not fray.

Simultaneous strip patch work and quilting (Christine Cooper)

This is a good way of making a quick and economical quilt, for the strip method uses up all the odd bits of fabric and if the strips are applied to a padded background the piecing and the quilting are achieved at the same time.

Preparation

Decide on the number and size of squares that will be needed. Cut that number of squares in 2oz (60g) polyester wadding and in backing fabric – which could be calico, cotton or old sheeting. Pin, and then tack the squares together, working from the backing side as this makes it easier to pull out the tacking threads afterwards.

Lattice strips and Border: cut the fabric for these on the straight grain, with a ¼in (6mm) seam allowance each side. The fabric could be the same as the backing fabric, or one of the fabrics used for the squares.

Squares: cut the strips on the straight grain with a seam allowance, making them as long as possible. Vary the widths if you wish.

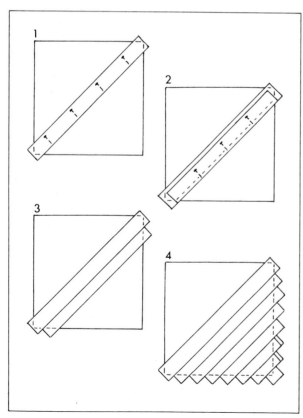

Method

1. Place the first strip right side up across the diagonal of a square, wadding side up. Pin in place. Cut to length. Repeat for all the squares using different fabrics from the colour scheme.
2. Lay the second strip face down on the first, raw edges matching, and using the side of the machine foot as a guide stitch through all layers. Use a thread to match the backing fabric. Cut strip to length. Repeat for all squares.
3. Open out the second strip and place the third strip face down on top, raw edges matching. Stitch along the seam line. Repeat for all the squares.
4. Continue working in this way until the corner is reached – as the lengths needed become shorter use up the smaller pieces of fabric rather than cutting them off the longer lengths.

Repeat for the second half of each square. Working on all the squares in sequence enables the fabric to be spread throughout all the squares, and also allows for new fabric to be introduced without spoiling the project should supplies run out.

Assembly

Trim the squares to size.

Arrange them in a pleasing pattern.

Stitch them together in horizontal rows, wrong sides together. Trim seams. Press.

Press under small turnings on the lattice strips. Centre the strips over the raw edges of the seams on the right side, pin in place and cut lattice to length. Machine close to both outer edges through all layers. Repeat until all the short lattice strips are in place.

Join the rows of squares together, wrong sides facing. Cover each seam with a lattice strip before adding the next row of squares.

Finishing

Add a border (see section on Borders, page 68), or finish the edges as described on page 110. This patchwork does not need to be lined as there are no raw edges.

Opposite: **A strip quilt.** *Worked by the simultaneous strip patchwork and quilting method, the lattice strips and the border match the backing fabric (Christine Cooper).*

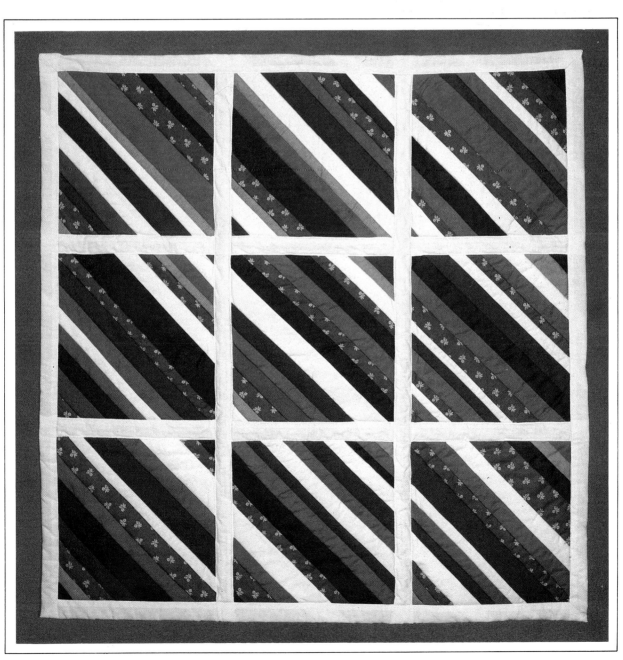

Seminole patchwork

This patchwork is an extension of strip piecing developed by the Seminole Indians of Florida. Fabric strips of varying widths are machined together, then cut into sections and resewn to make strips of patterns. The Seminoles used this technique to insert strips of brilliant colour into the plain fabric of shirts, skirts and dresses. Their method has now been adapted for use in quilts and other articles, using silks and patterned fabrics as well as thin cottons.

Design ideas

For dress the Seminole patchwork is usually on a small scale with the strips varying in width from ¾in (18mm) to 1½in (36mm) including a ¼in (6mm) seam. Furnishings and quilts use Seminole patchwork on a larger scale, the strips being 3in (7.5cm) wide or more.

The rows of joined strips can be cut and re-arranged to produce an endless variety of patterns. Some of these are illustrated in the diagrams.

Preparation

Cut the strips on the straight grain of the fabric, allowing ¼in (6mm) each side for seams. Make the strips longer than you think you will need as there is wastage when re-cutting. Pin the strips at intervals along one edge, right sides together.

Sewing and Finishing

Stitch along the seam line and press the seam to one side. When three or four strips have been sewn together, cut across them according to the diagrams

and re-sew, again with a ¼in (6mm) seam. Two or more different patterned strips can be used in the same piece of work, separated by one or more strips of plain fabric.

The finished patchwork should be lined.

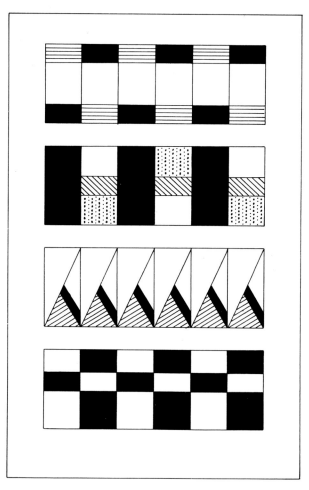

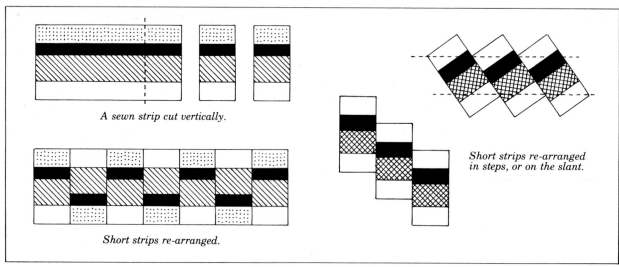

A sewn strip cut vertically.

Short strips re-arranged.

Short strips re-arranged in steps, or on the slant.

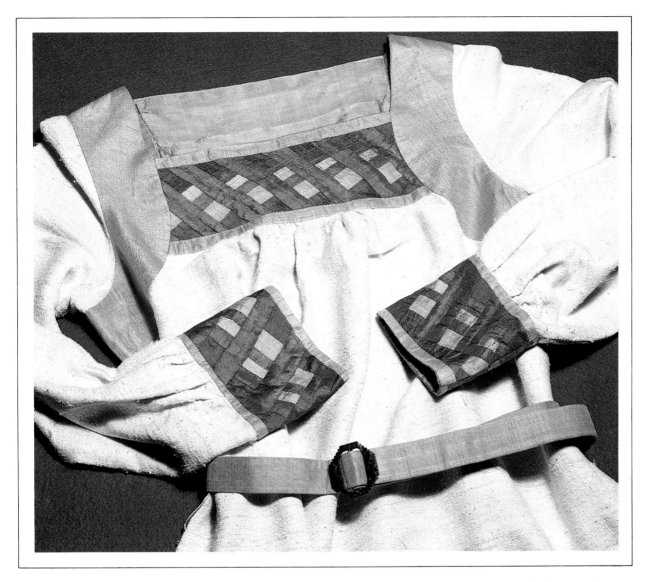

Seminole yoke and cuffs. *A wild silk dress decorated with Seminole Indian patchwork on cuffs and yoke in Thai silks. The shot fabrics contribute greatly to the finished effect, giving subtle contrast of tone instead of the traditionally bold colour contrasts* (Valerie Tulloch).

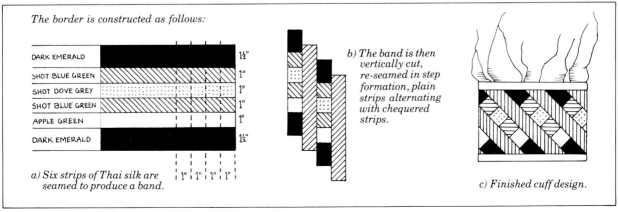

The border is constructed as follows:

DARK EMERALD	1½"
SHOT BLUE GREEN	1"
SHOT DOVE GREY	1"
SHOT BLUE GREEN	1"
APPLE GREEN	1"
DARK EMERALD	1½"

1" 1" 1" 1"

a) Six strips of Thai silk are seamed to produce a band.

b) The band is then vertically cut, re-seamed in step formation, plain strips alternating with chequered strips.

c) Finished cuff design.

Block patchwork with Seminole borders

Construction of block

The simplest method of joining is to sew it into three horizontal rows, 1–7, 8–17 and 18–24, and then join the rows into one block.

Above: **Place mat.** *The centre of this mat is a nine-patch block 'Card trick'. The borders are Seminole patchwork (Pamela Greaves).*

Seminole border

Four strips 1½in (37mm) wide are seamed together. This strip is then cut into sections as shown in the diagram, and the sections are re-arranged, seamed together as a band, and used as a border each end of the block.

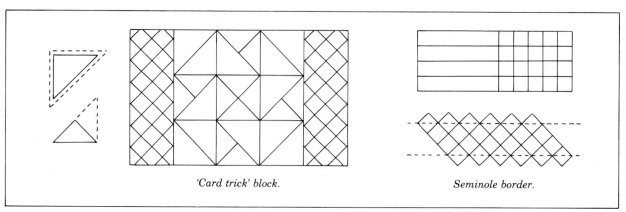

'Card trick' block.   *Seminole border.*

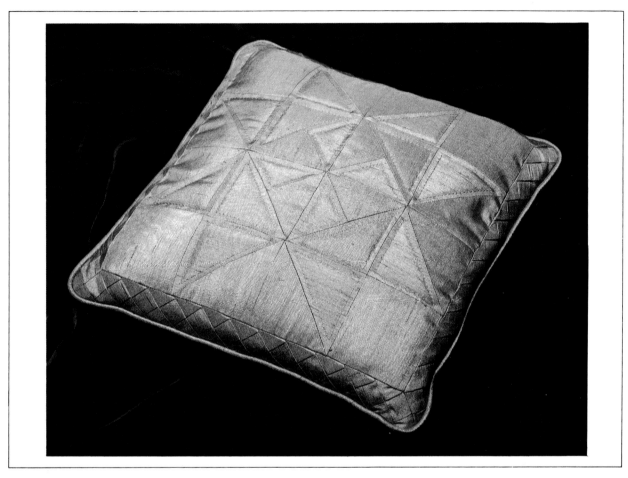

Above: **Shot silk cushion with Seminole
border.** *The cushion is 14½in (37cm) square,
and consists of a 12in (30cm) 'Martha
Washington' block with a 1¼in (3cm) wide
Seminole border* (Pamela Watts).

Construction of block

The block is machine-pieced. The grain of the shot
tussah silk is arranged as shown by the arrows, to
give variation in tone and colour.

Quilting

Hand-quilted, in the hand, using silk twist thread.
The design was transferred with a water-soluble
marking pen.

Seminole border

Machine-pieced in the same fabric. The two outer
strips of fabric are 1½in (4.5cm) wide, the central
piece is 1¼in (3cm) wide. Cut the sewn horizontal
strips into 1¼in (3cm) vertical strips, and rejoin
at an angle.

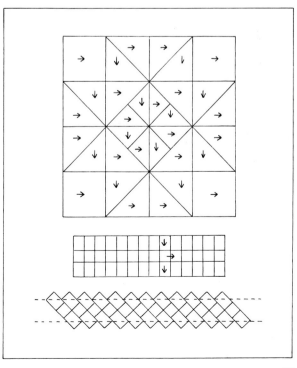

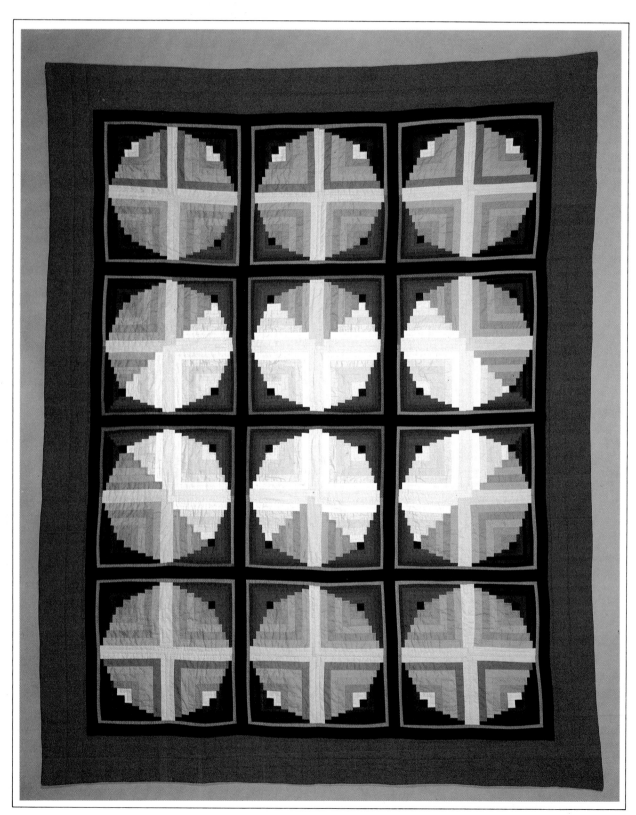

Log Cabin patchwork – pieced

(for Applied Log Cabin see pages 38–41)

This method is used when the patchwork is to be quilted, as it has no backing and is less bulky.

There are two sequences of sewing the strips to the central square which are described in the section on Applied Log Cabin, so only one method is described here.

Cutting out

Cut squares of fabric for the centre of each block. These can be any size but a usual one is 1½in–2in (3.5cm–4cm).

Mark strips on a fabric with a pencil and ruler, following the grain of the fabric. Allow ¼in (6mm) seam allowance on each side. These strips can be anything from ¾in (18mm) upwards, but a usual one is 1½in–2in (3.5cm–4cm) wide. Cut out accurately.

Method

1. Cut one strip the same length as one side of the central square. Lay it face down on the square, matching raw edges. Pin at right angles to the edge. Stitch ¼in (6mm) in from the edge. Fold back to the right side and press flat.
2. Cut the next strip the length of one side of the square plus the width of the first strip. Lay face down matching raw edges, pin and stitch.
3. Continue in this manner working clockwise around the central square (4) until the required size is reached (5).

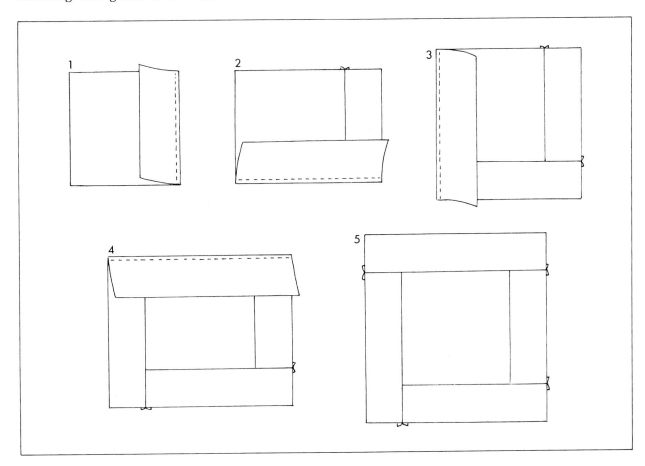

Opposite: **Log Cabin quilt – pieced.** *A machine-pieced quilt built up from thick and thin strips which give a circular effect. Hand-quilted* (Louise Bartlett).

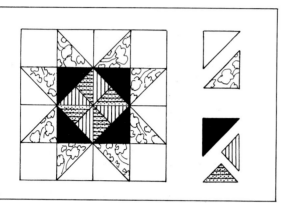

Below: **Cushion.** *Made from furnishing fabric remnants. 'Martha Washington Star' block, 16in (40cm) square. A four-patch block of 4in (10cm) squares with two templates. Join the patches into squares, sew the squares into four vertical rows, join the rows into a block. Hand-quilted ¼in (6mm) from seam line (Doreen Harding).*

Block patterns

The early American quilt-makers developed the block patterns, which used up scraps of fabrics and enabled a large patchwork to be made relatively easily in cramped living conditions. They developed the patterns by folding squares of paper, then cutting out the shapes and using these for templates. A single block pattern is usually square and made up of geometric shapes.

When a number of blocks is set (joined) together a variety of patterns is made. The simple shapes and straight seams make them ideal for machine patchwork. Block patterns can usually be divided into categories based on the number of squares into which a block can be divided.

Number of squares

It is useful for the quilt-maker to recognise these categories because construction is then easier to understand. The *four-patch* is the simplest. The block is divided into four equal squares – and includes blocks with multiples of four, sixteen and sixty-four squares.

The *nine-patch* is best known, and also includes blocks divided into thirty-six squares. The *five-patch* is divided into twenty-five squares and the *seven-patch* has forty-nine squares.

Size

When you are choosing a block pattern, make sure that it is suitable for the size of the project, for in machine patchwork the patches themselves should not be too small and fiddly to sew. Start with a simple block pattern such as the Martha Washington Star, which could be made up into a cushion like the one illustrated here.

A cot quilt could be a simple four-patch block repeated, such as the Windmill block shown here, each block about 8in (20cm) square. You will need twenty blocks, four across and five down.

Most blocks on full-sized patchwork quilts measure about 12in (30cm) square. If you are designing a bed quilt it is a good idea to make enough blocks to cover the top of the bed, then use a plain border to hand over the sides, and finish with a narrow patchwork strip around the edges. Plain or patchwork borders are useful for making up the project to the required size, and they help to frame the design.

Another way of increasing the area of your patchwork without making more blocks is to set the blocks with lattice strips. These frame the individual blocks and are also a useful way of harmonising a scrap quilt. Alternating pieced blocks with plain squares is yet another method.

A simple four-patch block, containing 16 squares.

Four blocks set together. Notice a new pattern appearing.

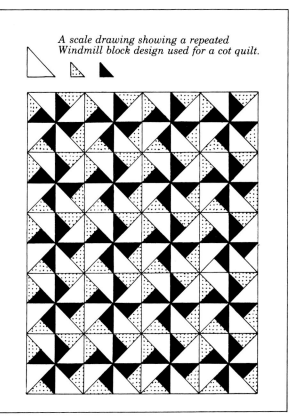

A scale drawing showing a repeated Windmill block design used for a cot quilt.

Preparation

When all the patches have been cut, lay out the design. Although it will not fit together very well, it enables you to check for design mistakes which are easier to rectify at this stage.

Seam allowance

Machine patchwork depends on lining up the edge of the patches with the outer edge of the presser foot. On most machines this gives a ¼in (6mm) seam allowance. If it does not, mark the measurement on the place with masking tape and align the fabric against the edge. Keep a constant seam allowance throughout the project, otherwise the patches will not fit together accurately.

Sewing

Tacking is unnecessary. Pin the patches right sides together, keeping the pins horizontal to the edge being sewn. Set the machine to about 5 stitches per 10cm and use a neutral-colour thread. Feed the patches carefully through the machine, removing the pins before they go under the pressure foot. Begin and end with a couple of back stitches to prevent the ends unravelling.

Pressing

Always press connecting seams open before joining the next patch. Because machine stitches are much stronger than those sewn by hand, press all the seams open throughout the patchwork in order to reduce bulk and make it easier to match aligning seams.

Press first on the back, then on the front, using a pressing cloth to prevent glazing.

Construction

Join the smallest unit together first, then join them into rows and finally sew the rows together. Pin both sides of matching seams to keep them in position, and ease in any fullness with pins. A large quilt can be completed in thirds, which are then joined.

Lattice strips

Using lattice strips is a useful way of making up a patchwork quickly with fewer blocks. They are added when the blocks are completed.

One set of strips should be cut to the height of a block (including seam allowances) and a second set should measure the width of a row (which
continued on page 62

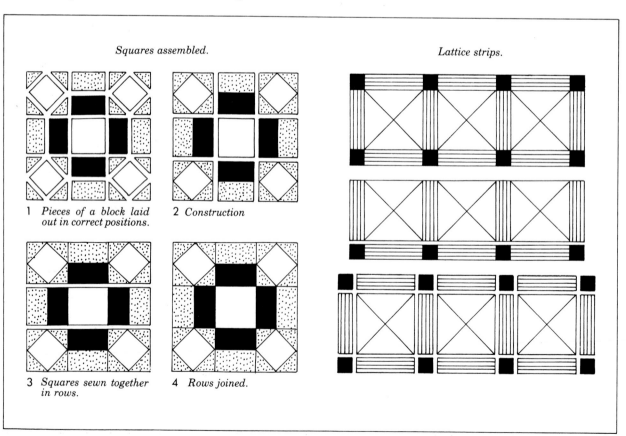

Squares assembled.

1 *Pieces of a block laid out in correct positions.*

2 *Construction*

3 *Squares sewn together in rows.*

4 *Rows joined.*

Lattice strips.

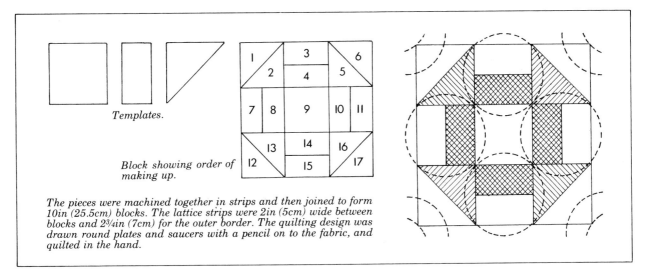

Templates.

Block showing order of making up.

The pieces were machined together in strips and then joined to form 10in (25.5cm) blocks. The lattice strips were 2in (5cm) wide between blocks and 2¾in (7cm) for the outer border. The quilting design was drawn round plates and saucers with a pencil on to the fabric, and quilted in the hand.

Below: **Class quilt.** *Worked by the members of a beginners' class, made in cotton, machine-pieced and hand-quilted. 'Shermans' March' block, with one variation – the outer corners of the corner blocks are squares instead of two triangles, owing to shortage of material. Overall measurements 39½in x 51in (103cm x 130cm). Design repeated twelve times, and linked by lattice strips (owned by Ruth Facey).*

includes the blocks and strips sewn together). Sew all the blocks together in rows, alternating blocks and strips of lattice, then join the rows together with the long lattice strips between each.

Design

Planning your patchwork is very important. This means working out the size, pattern, colours and finally, fabrics.

One way of designing is to work on graph paper with coloured pens or pencils using a 1cm square for each square in a block. Choose a block you like, then set four together and colour in the shapes. The blocks can also be set diagonally but extra half-blocks are needed to fill in the edges. Since some people find designing with coloured pencils difficult to relate to the final choice of fabrics, an alternative method is to cut out small squares of fabric and stick them on to graph paper – this allows greater flexibility in designing, although the fabric patterns will not be to the scale of the final patch size.

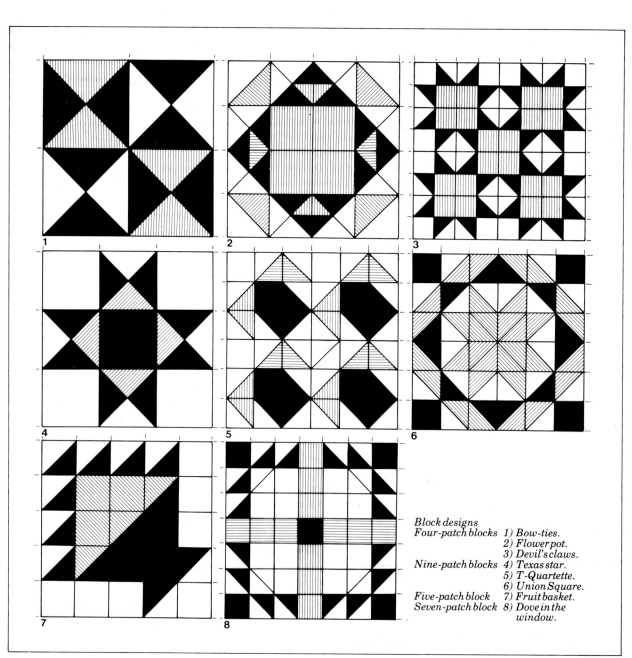

Block designs
Four-patch blocks 1) *Bow-ties.*
        2) *Flower pot.*
        3) *Devil's claws.*
Nine-patch blocks 4) *Texas star.*
        5) *T-Quartette.*
        6) *Union Square.*
Five-patch block 7) *Fruit basket.*
Seven-patch block 8) *Dove in the*
        window.

Make a design to scale

Whatever pattern you choose, make a design to scale on graph paper which shows the size of each patch, the number of blocks, borders, and colours.

From this you can estimate templates and fabrics and use it as a guide to making up the patchwork. It is important to work out your project thoroughly before embarking on cutting fabrics and sewing, and the extra time spent in such planning will make the following stages easier and quicker to accomplish.

Garden bench cushion

This is composed of four blocks each 12in (30cm) square in traditional 'Variable Star' design. A similar layout could be used for a long window seat, or a bedhead.

The blocks are joined in line, and a border made of 2in (5cm) squares pieced into strips is added separately. The quilting is by hand, the design being marked with a water-soluble pen. The patchwork is made into a box cushion and piped. See diagrams and photograph below (Vida James).

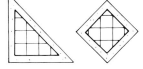

Draw out the block to the finished size (without seam allowances).

Glue shapes to card or sandpaper, add ¼in (6mm) seam all round.

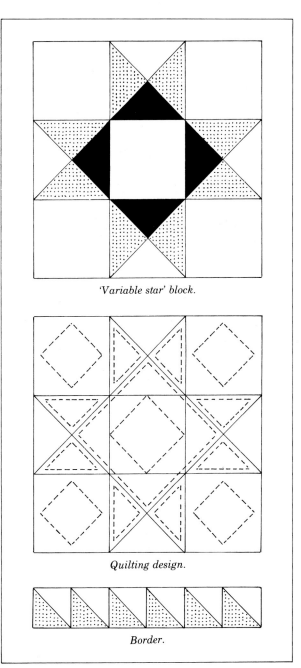

'Variable star' block.

Quilting design.

Border.

Templates

Templates are made when the design and the size of the work has been decided. Templates are needed for each individual shape within a design. They must be very accurate because they are the shapes from which the fabric patches are cut, and if they are even slightly incorrect this will accumulate over a number of patches.

Templates for machine patchwork must include the size of the finished patch and a ¼in (6mm) seam allowance on all edges. (This seam allowance is predetermined by the presser foot.) To guarantee accuracy, draw out the block to be used on graph paper, using a metal ruler and a well-sharpened 2H pencil. Carefully cut out the different shapes that are needed, using the metal ruler and a scalpel knife. Stick them on thick card or sandpaper – sandpaper does not wear so well but it adheres to the fabric better than card – and then add ¼in (6mm) seam allowance on all sides and cut out. Window templates are useful in framing a particular area of fabric to be used. Make them in the usual way, but cut out the centre around the edge of the finished size.

Estimating fabrics

It is important to be able to estimate accurately the amount of fabric required, and this can only be done when the templates have been made and the number of patches calculated. Always include seam allowances. Estimating fabric depends on how many times a template can be laid across a width of fabric, selvedge to selvedge. Always place as many edges of the template as possible either on the straight grain which runs parallel to the selvedge, or on the cross-grain. Avoid the bias, which has the most stretch, as much as possible. Divide the total number of patches by the number fitted across a width of fabric, then multiply that number by the width of the template. Butt the templates together, leaving no space in between.

Estimate in this way for each different template and type of fabric used. Also, use the width of the fabric as a guideline for estimating borders and lattice strips. It is wise to add 10in (25cm) extra for safety.

Marking and cutting fabrics

Always wash the fabrics, if necessary, and iron them flat before use.

Mark the fabrics on the reverse side with a well-sharpened coloured pencil – never use biros or felt-tip pens which will stain the fabric and templates.

To stop the fabric from slipping, lay it over an old sheet or suchlike. Try and match the fabric grain to the edge of the template.

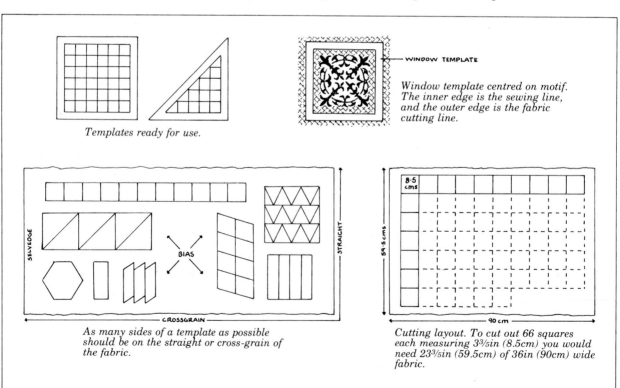

Templates ready for use.

WINDOW TEMPLATE

Window template centred on motif. The inner edge is the sewing line, and the outer edge is the fabric cutting line.

As many sides of a template as possible should be on the straight or cross-grain of the fabric.

Cutting layout. To cut out 66 squares each measuring 3⅗in (8.5cm) you would need 23⅗in (59.5cm) of 36in (90cm) wide fabric.

Mark around each template carefully, for a good result depends on accurate marking and cutting. No seam-lines are drawn. Avoid the selvedges which are often marked and uneven.

Cut each patch out separately. Fabric used for borders can be torn *if the grain is straight*, but check this before you tear any large amounts.

Star pattern cushion
(see below and overleaf)

One plain and one flowered fabric were used for the star, which was pieced into a plain dark fabric to make up the square.

The block uses a single diamond template and

is made up as follows:
Pieces 1–4, 5–8, 9–12 and 13–16 are joined into strips, and these strips are joined to form a pieced diamond. Make up eight of these. Join block A to B, C to D, E to F and G to H, then sew these four pairs of diamonds together. Complete the star by joining together the two blocks of four diamonds. Finally, add the outer four triangles and squares.

Quilting

Templates were made of the quilting designs, which were transferred to the fabric with a chalk pencil, and quilted by hand, in a hoop. (Anne Sellars)

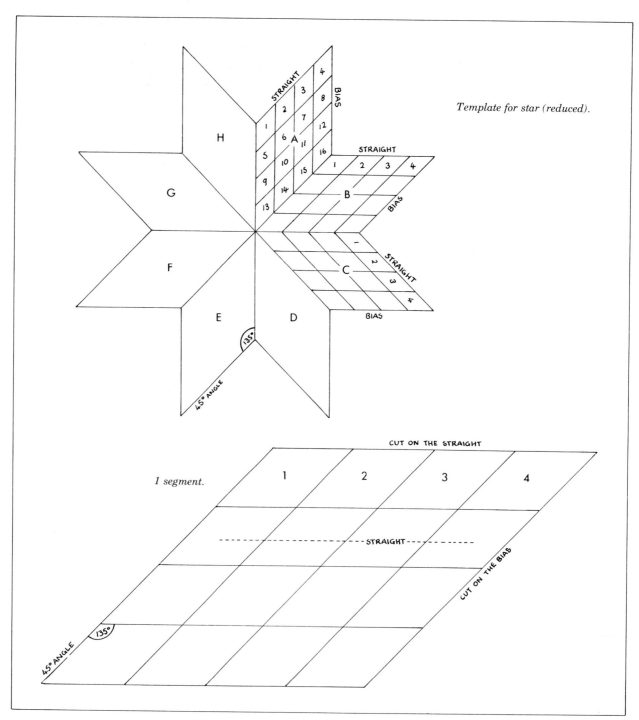

Template for star (reduced).

Templates of quilting patterns.

Borders

A border should be considered part of the original design. It can consist of plain strips or of patchwork. A border looks neater if the seams within it align with those in the main patchwork. This is particularly important when several lengths of plain fabric are joined together. If a patchwork border is used it needs to flow evenly around the main design since patches should not be cut to odd shapes in order to fit in. Turning corners is particularly difficult. It is often easier to consider these as separate squares.

The Wild Goose Chase border is an example of one that can change directions at the corner and centre.

Making up borders

Patchwork may not keep exactly to the original size, for fabrics often stretch, especially around the edges. It is important when making up borders, however, to refer back to the original design for the size, and to make the patchwork fit either by easing in fullness or slightly stretching. This ensures that the borders lie flat and the overall size is not uneven.

Borders can be attached in several ways. The simplest method is to make two strips corresponding to the lengths of the patchwork (remember to include seam allowances in all measurements). Join these to the sides, using the same sewing method as the main patchwork. Then cut two strips corresponding to the width of the patchwork and of the strips on each side: join these to the top and bottom. Press the seams open.

Simple straight-cut borders are the easiest way to frame a patchwork.

Separate corner squares

Another method is to make the borders with separate corner squares. Four strips are made to correspond to the sides of the patchwork, and four squares to correspond to the width of the strips. The strips are joined in the same order as the previous method, but the top and bottom strips include a square at each end.

Contrasting squares add interest to the corners.

Mitred corners

Mitred corners are an elegant way to complete a plain border, or they can be used on bias strips or self-binding edges.

Make two strips the length of the patchwork plus two widths of the strip, and two further strips the width of the patchwork plus two widths of the strip.

Attach them in the usual way, first to the sides, then to the top and bottom, letting the ends extend to the corners. On the top and bottom strips in each of the four corners make a diagonal fold from the inside to the outer corner. Press the fabric under and hand-sew to the strip beneath.

Mitred corners are a simple but effective method of completing a plain border.

Opposite: **Medallion wall hanging** *made in pure cotton and 35in (89cm) square. The centre medallion is based on the 'Ohio Star' block. The borders are formed with two plain strips and a border of triangles, followed by two more strips.*

The rest of the hanging is made with strips of various widths ending with one broad band. All machine-pieced.

Quilting: The broad band is quilted with a 'Goose Wing' design. A cardboard template was used, laid on the fabric and marked round with a 2H pencil – the centre being joined up freehand. Outline quilting was worked in the centre. All the quilting was done by hand in a large hoop(Ann Ohlenschlager).

Goosewing template, 10½in × 4in (26.5cm × 10cm).

Below: **Pinwheel design cushion.** *This block is also known as 'Prairie Windmill'. Machine pieced and hand quilted. Eight triangles surround an octogon, and one half triangle at each corner forms a square. The base of each triangle is three times longer than each side of the octogon* (Pamela Greaves).

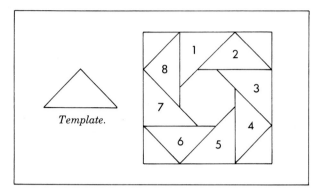

Template.

Below: **Quilt-carrying bag.** *Overall dimensions
– 16in × 20in (40.5cm × 15cm), with an 8in
(20cm) gusset at the sides and an 8in (20cm)
base. Made in cottons – dark brown, yellow ochre
and yellow floral. Machine pieced and quilted in
fourteen 8in (20cm) square blocks, with a 3in
(7.5cm) band round the top, and handles 1½in
(3.5cm) wide. 'Pin Wheel' block. When the blocks
are joined two complete pinwheels are formed,
one in dark brown and one in ochre* (Ann
Ohlenschlager).

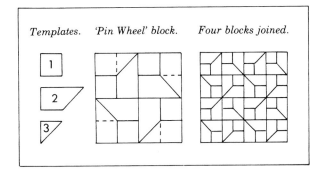

Machine-piecing a curved seam

Piecing a pattern with curved seams requires a little more time and care than straight seams, but the following method will produce a neat join:

1. Make card templates as usual, including ¼in (6mm) seam on all edges.

   Draw around the template on to the fabric with the grain of the fabric along the straight sides of the templates.

   Add balance marks at the centre points. Cut fabric shapes out carefully and accurately.

2. Hold the straight edges together at each end and pin, weaving the pin in and out twice for security.

3. Hold the fabric pieces right sides together. Place a pin at the balance marks.

4. Pin twice more in between, easing the circular shape into the L shape. Sew with a ¼in (6mm) seam using the side of the presser foot as a guide. Press the seam allowance as it falls naturally, usually towards the concave side of the curve.

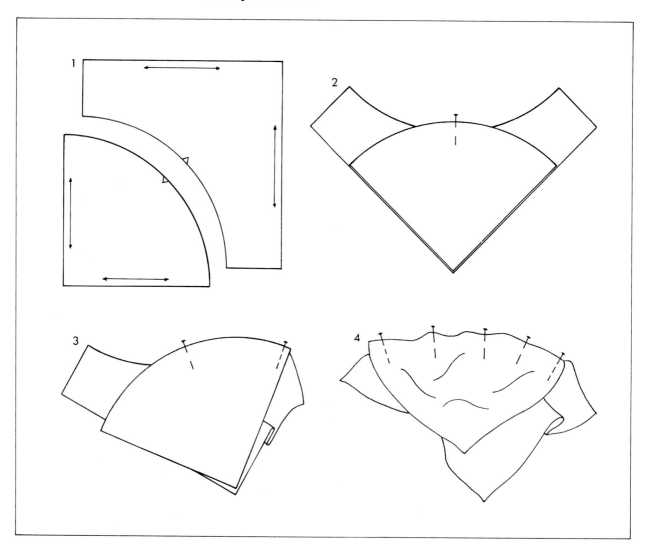

Opposite: **Cot Quilt.** *An example of a simple curved-seam repeating pattern made interesting by subtle variations in colour, achieved by home dyeing* (Valerie Campbell-Harding).

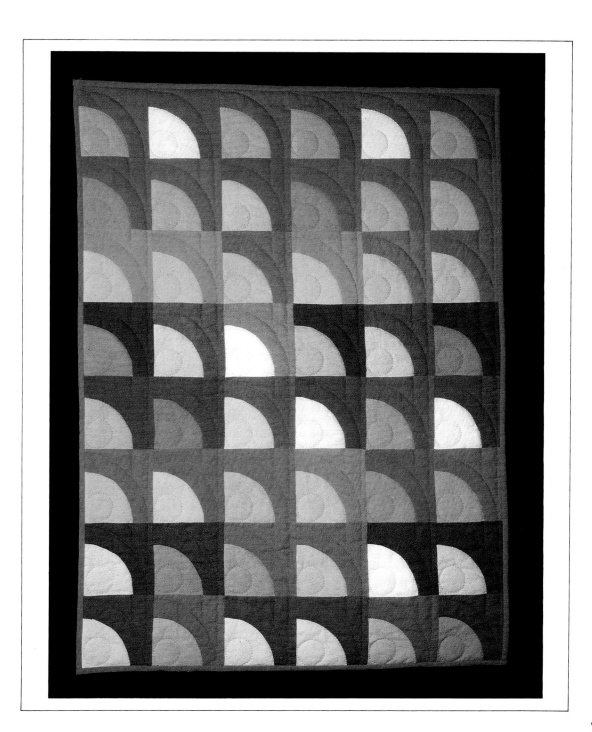

Stuffed patchwork

Patchwork can be made into raised or three-dimensional shapes and stuffed to give added warmth, body, or for textural effect. Free standing objects such as toys or cushions are also stuffed.

The simplest method is to sew two shapes together with the right sides inside, and then turn the right sides out, stuff, and slip-stitch the opening to secure it. This method gives a shape that is raised in the middle and flatter at the edges, as a cushion is. For a more tailored look a gusset should be included between the two shapes, but this is tricky when the article is small. Spherical objects made of oversewn patchwork should be made in two halves, and then joined.

Different stuffings are used for different purposes. The most useful is a terylene toy stuffing which is light and springy and washes well. If this is not available terylene wadding can be used shredded into small pieces.

For a flat shape (such as the hammock on page 79) a strip of wadding can be pulled through each fabric tube and slip-stitched. A single nylon stocking can be used for puff patchwork, but nylon is too heavy when used in bulk. Shredded foam pieces are cheap but look lumpy. A single shape cut from foam plastic is perfectly satisfactory as a toy, for example, and is used for the dog shown opposite.

The best stuffing for cushions is feathers, which are very long-lasting.

Kapok can be packed to make something that is really tight when stuffed, as toys are, but if it is left at all loose it will go into lumps.

Method for pincushion. *Sew the two short sides together. Stitch straight across one long side. Open the 'bag' and centre the open end of the short seam in the middle of the other side of the bag and stitch across, leaving a small opening for the stuffing. Stuff firmly, then oversew the opening.*

This shape only works if the width of the strip is less than half the length, and it looks most effective if the fabric is brightly striped. This accentuates the shape.

Opposite: **Dog.** *Made in a variety of cottons by the oversewn method, using a 1in (25mm) template. The papers were removed before the toy was made up. The filling is a piece of thick plastic foam, cut slightly larger than the shape to give a firm fit (Frances Collins).*

Opposite: **Pig.** *Made in felt, the body consists of twelve pentagons oversewn together – make it in two halves and join them – leave a small slit and fill with wadding. The legs are rolled strips of felt and the nose is three applied circles. The tail is stiffened with wire (Jill Pickup).*

Opposite: **Pincushion.** *Made of striped cotton material in the shape of an old-fashioned 'humbug' sweet. Cushions can also be made like this, using striped material. The pincushion is made of a strip of fabric 4in × 11in (10cm × 28cm), and a cushion strip would measure 10in × 26½in (25cm × 67cm) (Valerie Campbell-Harding).*

Left: **Pomander.** *Pentagons of lawn and lace were sewn together by the oversewn method and formed into a ball. Before being filled with potpourri, the papers were taken out, so that the fragrance could come through the openwork lace. The pomander is trimmed with pearls and finished with a ribbon* (Brenda Showler).

Below: **Hanging pincushion.** *Two traditional flower shapes in hexagons in soft cottons, worked by the oversewn method, joined together and stuffed to make a pincushion* (Bridget Ingram).

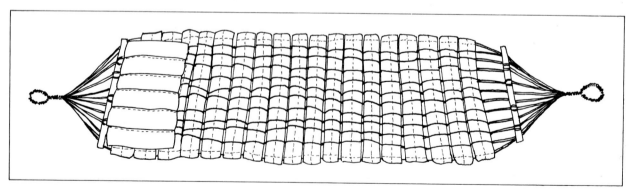

Opposite and above: **Hammock.** *This consists of tubular strips of patchwork sewn by machine, and stuffed with a strip of wadding pulled through each fabric tube, giving a flat padded effect. These strips were then joined with machine-stitching, making a mattress shape, which was woven through with cord joined to wooden stretchers each end to make the hammock* (Valerie Campbell-Harding).

Raised patchwork

Raised patchwork is made by stuffing double-sided shapes with wadding. These are then joined to make flat articles such as quilts, or more firmly stuffed for three-dimensional shapes.

Design ideas

All kinds of geometric shapes may be used, as well as free shapes such as flower petals. Stuffed shapes can be built up into three-dimensional pieces such as the pincushions shown here, flowers, Christmas tree ornaments and toys.

Preparation

Make a card template of the shape required, including a ¼in (6mm) seam allowance. Lay this template on the wrong side of the fabric, and draw around the shape. Draw two pieces for every finished patch. Cut around the shapes.

Sewing

Place two pieces face to face and seam around them, but leaving a small opening. Turn inside out. Stuff lightly with wadding. Slip stitch the opening together. When a number of patches have been made they can be joined by oversewing or bagotting.

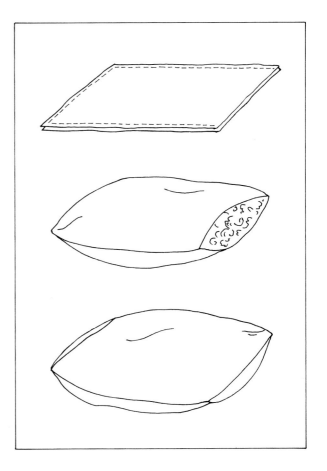

Opposite and above: **Flower pincushions.**
(Valerie Campbell-Harding).

Puff patchwork

Puff patchwork is basically square or rectangular bags of fabric stuffed with wadding, and sewn together. The back is flat, the front very raised.

It is a quick method of making a warm quilt, but it can also be used for cushions or bags. Cotton fabric is best.

Design ideas

The squares or rectangles can be of different sizes, as long as they all fit together without gaps. Rectangles can be arranged to make chevron patterns as in parquet flooring. If the squares are all the same size, colour can be used to make a pattern such as checkerboard or Greek crosses.

If transparent fabric is used for the top layer, the filling can be coloured to make a delicate colour scheme, for example, for a pram cover.

Preparation

Cut one 2in (5cm) square and one 2½in (7.5cm) square of fabric. Place the wrong sides together and pin at the corners. Pleat the excess fabric at the centre of the sides and pin the layers together. Prepare a number of these.

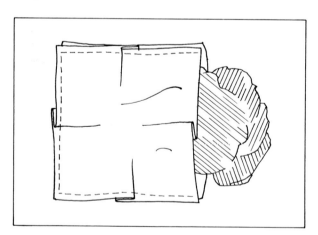

Sewing and Finishing

Stitch around three sides of each square, preferably by machine, leaving a ¼in (6mm) seam. Insert wadding, scraps or a nylon stocking through the opening, being careful not to stuff too tightly. Make a pleat on the fourth side and stitch it closed. When a number of puffs have been made, place them face to face and stitch them together over the previous seam.

Press the seams open. Back the puffs with a piece of plain fabric and bind the edges with narrow strips of fabric.

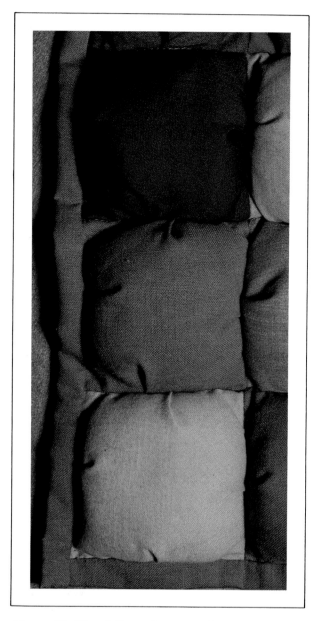

Above: **Puff patchwork cot quilt.** *Corner of a quilt in two colours (Valerie Campbell-Harding).*

Opposite: **Cushion of interlocked rings.** *Strips of cotton about 4in (10cm) wide and of different lengths were machined together to form tubes and stuffed. Each 'ring' is about 3ft (1m) long (Valerie Campbell-Harding).*

82

Folded & Gathered patchwork

The methods which follow give texture to patchwork but, because of the layers of fabric, they are not quilted. Thin fabrics such as silk, lawn or dress cottons should be used to avoid too much bulk and for easier handling. If you wish to make a larger article with thick fabrics, then the size of each piece should be larger in proportion.

These methods use squares, rectangles and circles of fabric, which are then folded or gathered in various ways to produce smaller shapes. Because these shapes are geometric they can be put together in an unlimited number of ways to make patterns. Although the finished patchwork is usually made up of a single method or shape, many colours can be used to make quite complicated patterns.

The finished shapes are usually joined by hand, though some methods have now been developed using machine stitching.

Folded and gathered patchwork techniques are not usually combined with flat patchwork because of the different thicknesses, though it is possible to do this if the flat areas are backed or quilted to give them body.

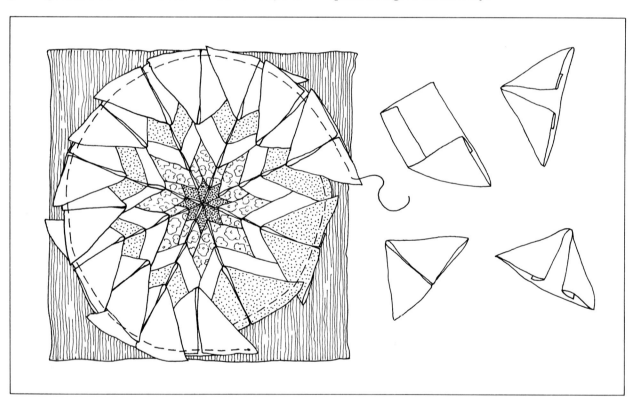

Illustrated sample of Somerset patchwork or 'Folded stars'.

Opposite: **Wall hanging with Catherine wheel design.** *Somerset patchwork in cotton fabrics, in which new colours are introduced with each increase in the number of patches. Finished into a square, with Log Cabin patchwork border, edged with folded patches (Azalea Mayhew).*

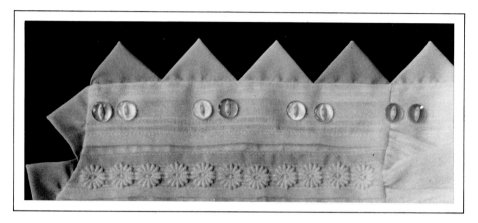

Ribbon edge. *Ribbon used to make a folded edging, designed for a housecoat* (Valerie Campbell-Harding).

Below: **Somerset patchwork samples.** *These show different arrangements of fabrics, colours and triangles* (Valerie Campbell-Harding).

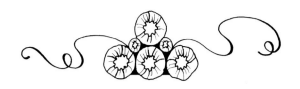

Folded stars or Somerset patchwork

This is a form of patchwork using either squares or strips of fabric or ribbon, folded to make triangles. These triangles are then sewn to a backing fabric to make patterns of stars or crosses, or they are inserted into a seam or an edge as borders. They can be sewn by hand or machine or a combination of both. A fine fabric should be used that creases easily and is not springy.

Method 1

Cut a 2in (5cm) square of fabric. Fold in half diagonally to form a triangle. Fold again diagonally to make a smaller triangle. Press.

Make a number of these.

To make a border. Start at the folded edge of one of the triangles and tack the raw edges together. When you are two-thirds of the way along insert another triangle and continue tacking. The result-ing length of triangles is then inserted in a seam.

If you wish to make a circular or square pattern follow the final instructions.

Method 2

Cut a 2in (5cm), or larger, square of fabric. Fold in half to make a rectangle. Fold the top corners to the centre of the base making a triangle. Press with your fingers or an iron. Make a number of these and sew to a foundation fabric as given in the final instructions.

Method 3

Cut a card template 2in × 1¼in (5.5cm × 3.5cm). Cut a rectangle of fabric using the template as a guide. Fold over ¼in (6mm) hem on one of the long sides of each piece and press between finger and thumb. Fold the top corners to the centre of the base making a triangle. Press.

Make a number of these and sew to a foundation fabric as given in the final instructions.

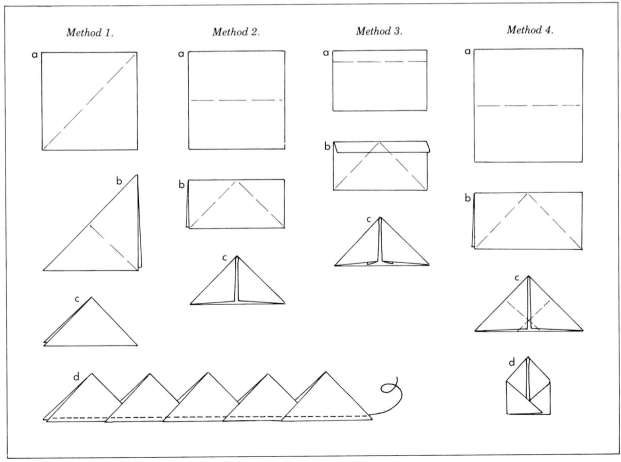

Method 1.   *Method 2.*   *Method 3.*   *Method 4.*

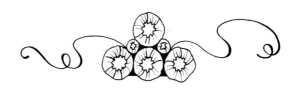

Method 4

Cut a 2in (5cm) or larger square of fabric. Fold in half to make a rectangle. Fold the top corners to the centre of the base making a triangle. Fold the side points in so that they overlap the centre fold making a pentagonal shape. Make a number of these.

Sewing the patterns

Mark a square on a piece of calico or old sheeting. The size can vary from 6in (15cm) to a size large enough for a whole cushion cover.

Draw diagonal lines from corner to corner, and vertical and horizontal lines from the centre of each side.

Circular patterns

Round 1. Take four triangles of the same colour and place them on the backing square with all four points touching at the centre. The backing fabric should not show.

Pin through all layers along the folds.

Sew each point to the backing with a tiny stitch. Then sew the raw edges down with either a running stitch or with a straight or zigzag machine stitch. Care must be taken to avoid the triangles shifting while you are sewing.

Round 2. Eight triangles of another colour are needed, and the points should be placed about ½in (1cm) away from the centre. Sew as before.

Round 3. Eight triangles of a third colour are needed for round 3, sixteen for rounds 4 and 5, 32

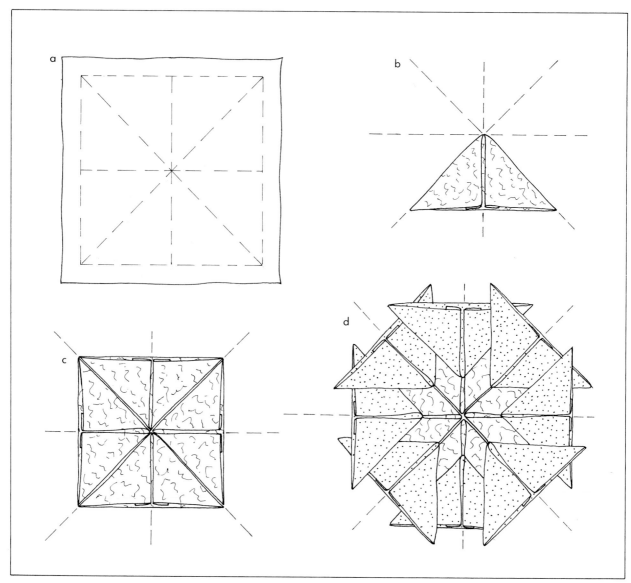

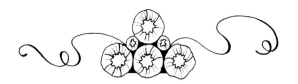

for rounds 6 and 7, and so on.

This will make a circular pattern. When finished this can be inserted into a slightly smaller hole in another fabric. The edges of the hole are turned under and hemmed through all the layers to hold them firmly and cover the raw edges. If you wish to make the circle fill a square then the corners can be filled in with more triangles.

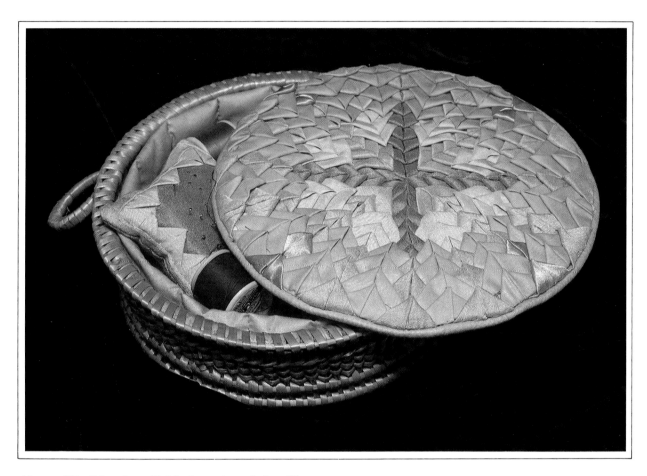

Above: **Workbasket.** *Folded patchwork in silks and cottons, placed alternately to give radiating effect* (Azalea Mayhew).

Square patterns

Sew four triangles as before with the points touching at the centre. Sew eight more in Round 2. Before the third round is added, four extra triangles are sewn at each corner. These extra triangles will be needed at least every alternate round, and sometimes between every round, depending on how you space the rounds. You should finish as a square each time, as the pattern keeps trying to make a circle.

Machine sewn method

Squares of fabric are folded in half to make rectangles. Two of these are placed on the backing square with the folded edges touching each other on a drawn line. Pin to the backing.

Machine a straight line down the centre of both squares.

Fold the top corners to the centre of the base making triangles, and pin.

Place two more squares on the backing in the spaces between the first two pieces and stitch as before. Fold corners as before and pin.

You will now have four triangles pinned to the backing. Be careful to cover the backing completely.

Zigzag around the raw edges through all the layers.

For the second and subsequent rounds do not sew right across the pieces, but only from the base to the point and back again.

Variations

These basic patterns can be varied in many ways, mainly by the placing of different colours within the rounds. Different sizes of triangles can be used in the same piece of work and the spacing between the rounds can vary.

This is essentially a method that develops as you work it, as it is extremely difficult to draw out any sort of pattern beforehand. You will gradually discover what sort of effects can be obtained when the colours are alternated in one round, or the triangles are placed on top of each other rather than in between. Folded triangles can be placed in a line rather than around a centre point, and built up with straight lines or curves of overlapping triangles. If two rows face each other the points of one row fit into the spaces of the other.

The folds of the fabric can be decorated with pintucks, lines of embroidery or overlocking stitch before the triangles are made. A striped or patterned fabric, or a border print, can be used. For texture the triangles can be made with frayed edges instead of folded ones, or the edge can be satin-stitched. The points can be left unstitched for a more raised effect.

Finishing

Strips of fabric can be sewn around these patterns to enlarge them for a bag or cushion, as in Log Cabin patchwork, or they can be sewn to each other to make a larger piece. The best way of doing this is to join two squares with a strip of fabric to avoid a bulky seam. Strips of joined squares can then be joined with a longer strip.

Quilting is not needed and anyway is not possible due to the thickness of the fabrics; but lining is necessary to hide the stitching on the back.

Opposite: **Somerset patchwork square** *in the centre of a cushion, surrounded by Log Cabin strips of different widths* (Valerie Campbell-Harding).

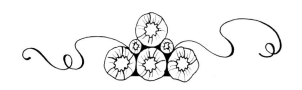

Cathedral window patchwork

Cathedral window patchwork differs from most other kinds in that it is three-dimensional and more solid in construction. It is generally made from doubled calico squares, pairs of which are joined with a seam which is covered with a small square of coloured cotton laid diagonally down the seam. Other fabrics such as satin, silk or patterned cotton can be used. The small squares can be of different fabrics and texture.

This patchwork can be sewn by hand or by machine.

Design ideas

The plain calico background has a unifying effect, so that small treasured scraps can be used for the coloured squares. The latter can also be embroidered with a single motif, or consist of pieces of canvas work, or fabric that has been stitched, dyed or painted.

The small squares of colour can be arranged in patterns such as diamonds or diagonal strips, or shaded from light to dark as in the jacket opposite. It is possible to use a single layer of leather instead of the doubled calico, turning the folds to show the suede on the reverse.

A row of tiny 'windows' can be used as a belt, a single one as a pocket, or two together as a pincushion.

BY HAND

Preparation

Cut a square of calico about four times as large as is required for the finished square – for example, cut an 8½in (21cm) square for a 4in (10cm) finished size. The sides should be on the straight grain of the fabric. Turn in a ¼in (6mm) hem all round the edge.

Fold each corner to the centre and pin. Again fold the corners to the centre and pin. Stitch all four corners together firmly, sewing through to the back.

Make a number of squares.

Sewing

Place two squares face to face with the folded edges level with each other, and oversew them together along one edge. Open them flat, and place them, smooth side down on a table.

Cut a 1¾in (4.3cm) square of coloured cotton and place it diagonally over the join. Roll the folds of calico back over the raw edges and hem them, or secure them with running stitch. This stitching should go right through to the back to hold all the layers together. Make rows of finished windows and then sew the rows together to make the article, adding more coloured squares between the rows.

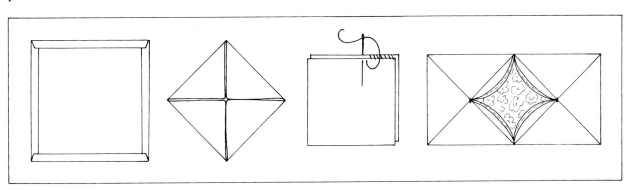

Opposite: **Jacket in Cathedral window patchwork.** *Worked by hand in calico, with central squares in four shades of brown velvet at the borders* (Christine Cooper).

Right: **Cathedral window pincushion.** *Two squares of cathedral window patchwork, made by the machine method, joined together and stuffed to make a pincushion* (Lois Hennequin).

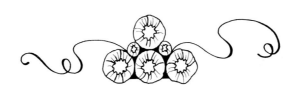

BY MACHINE

Before attempting this method, make a square by the hand method (page 93) so that the process is thoroughly understood. In the end, this method is quicker and easier, but it needs practice.

Preparation

Cut three card templates with the following measurements:
A. 9in (22.7cm) square
B. 4in × 8in (10cm × 20cm)
C. 2¼in (5.7cm) square

Sewing (see top diagrams next page)

Lay template A on the calico with the sides matching the grain, and draw around it with a hard pencil. Cut along the drawn line. Fold the piece in half. Place template B next to the fold and draw along the short edges only. Pin the layers together and seam along the short sides only. Trim the corners and press the seams open.

Bring the seams together with the right sides facing, and pin along the raw edges. Stitch, leaving an opening for turning. Clip the corners and press the seams open. Turn the square right side out, press flat, and slip-stitch the opening.

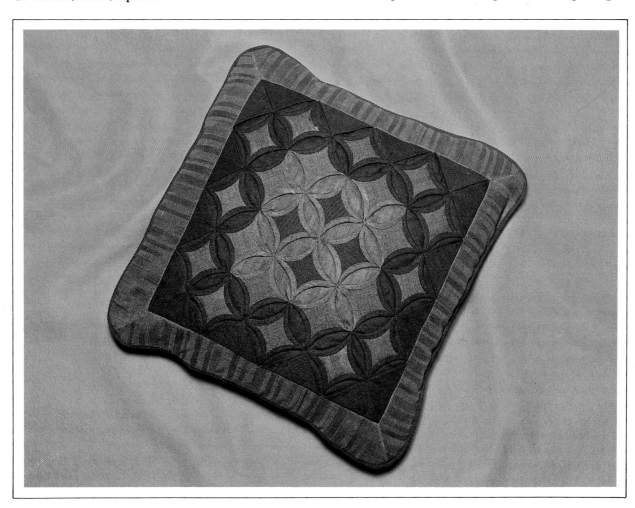

Above: **Cathedral window cushion.** *A subtle stained-glass effect is achieved in this cushion by the use of plain cottons combined with a striped satin weave fabric (Lynne Edwards).*

Opposite: **Cathedral window patchwork hanging.** *The large background squares of the hanging are composed of three layers, unbleached calico enclosing a layer of wadding. These squares were edge-stitched before the corners are folded to the centre and stitched.*

The smaller cathedral window motifs were attached to the centre squares before stitching the latter in place through the rolled over edges (Christine Cooper).

Bring corners 1 and 2 together and make a sharp fold (X) at the centre of each side. Draw lines from X to X on the seamed side of the square.

This is the seam line for joining the squares. Match the drawn lines on two squares, and stitch. Join a number of squares together in a row. Pin the four corners to the centre point of each square and stitch firmly together through all the layers.

Lay template C on the wrong side of the coloured cotton, draw around it and cut out. Place it diagonally over the exposed seam between two calico squares and pin through all the layers. Turn the edges back over the coloured area and hem, stitching through all the layers.

Finishing

No quilting, lining or edging is required, as this patchwork has no raw edges and is never less than two layers thick.

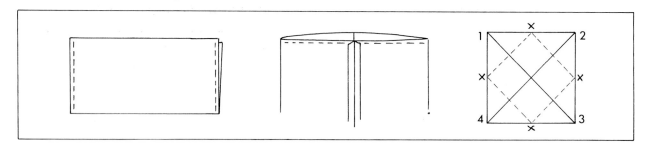

Suffolk puffs

These are gathered circular patches which are sewn together with spaces left between them. Fine fabrics should be used, such as silk, organdie and soft cottons. These make up into a delicate openwork fabric which is valued for decorative effect and textural qualities. The gathered side of the circles is the right side. In any one article the fabric should be of the same weight and type.

Design ideas

The design possibilities of Suffolk puffs are based on variations of colour and scale. Strips of puffs in different sizes or colours can be sewn together to make patterns such as diagonals, chevrons or squares. Tiny puffs can be used as decorative ends to ribbons. Areas of puffs will add texture to fashion designs such as sleeves on a wedding dress, but these should be in man-made fabrics as they cannot be ironed.

Small puffs can be placed inside large ones to add body and texture. It is also possible to pad or stuff the circles.

Toys can be made by threading puffs on to elastic or crochet cotton to make snakes, animals or dolls.

Preparation

Lay a small plate or saucer on the back of the chosen fabric, draw around it and cut out. The circle should be just over twice the size of the finished puff.

Sewing

Turn under a narrow hem on the wrong side and sew all around the circle with small running stitches. Draw the thread up tightly and finish off by oversewing two or three times in one place.

Join the patches together from the back (the smooth side) with a few stitches at four separate points around the edge. This turns the circle into a shape which is nearly square.

Finishing

The work may be left as it is, or backed with a fabric of a different colour which shows through the spaces.

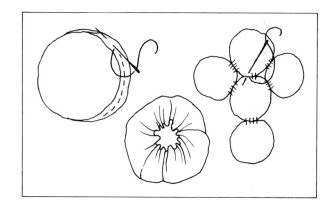

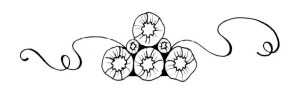

Below: **Suffolk puff pram cover.** *Two sizes of circles of cotton polyester voile were sprayed with fabric paint using an air brush. The edges were turned under and stitched, but a small circle of quilted wadding, covered with a piece of voile, was stitched in place in the centre of each circle before the edges were gathered. The puffs were mounted on a voile backing* (Pamela Watts).

Quilting and Finishing

Quilting gives extra warmth and decoration to patchwork, and all kinds of patchwork benefit from the extra weight and solidity given by even a minimal amount of quilting. The only kind of patchwork for which quilting is not recommended is some of the folded and gathered patchwork, which can be heavy enough on its own – although it is sometimes necessary to join linings with knotting or tufting.

Quilting is the sewing together of three layers, the patchwork top, the filling or wadding, and a backing fabric. It can be done by hand or by machine, but the filling and the technique varies according to the method used.

Design

Quilting gives a more interesting texture to the surface of the work, and adds to the overall effect. For this reason the quilting design should be considered at the design stage for the patchwork.

There are no design rules for quilting patchwork – but many traditional ways of working, as well as modern ideas.

'Contour' quilting has traditionally been used for block patterns, and it follows the shape of the patches about ¼in (6mm) from the seam lines.

Marking the fabric

If the quilting design needs to be marked on the patchwork it is much easier to do this before the three layers are tacked together. Work out your pattern on the original patchwork design to ensure that it fits.

Commercial stencils can be used, or the pattern can be marked out using a metre rule. Masking tape also makes a quick and effective guideline and, provided the design is worked out beforehand, can be applied when the work is in the hoop. Use a well-sharpened coloured pencil for marking the patchwork – a water-soluble blue pencil is now available, the marks of which can easily be dabbed out with a damp cloth.

Traditionally, quilting lines were often marked with a rug needle, held and pressed down firmly almost parallel to the work. This method works best on a padded surface and leaves an indented line when the needle is drawn firmly around the template – but remember, only work small areas at a time, for the indentation fades as the fabric is handled. The sections of the fabric can be marked by folding the work in quarters and pressing it.

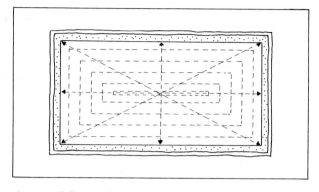

Assembly and tacking

Cut the wadding and backing fabric about 4in (10cm) bigger on all sides than the patchwork. This allows for shrinkage due to quilting and provides a self-binding if required.

Whether you quilt by hand or by machine, it is important to tack the layers thoroughly together. Lay the backing fabric on a flat surface, wrong side up, and stick the corners flat with masking tape. Lay the wadding on top, smooth it flat, then spread over the patchwork – right side up. Pin the three layers together, then tack, always working from the centre outwards to ease out any excess fabric. Cover the area thoroughly with an even distribution of tacking lines.

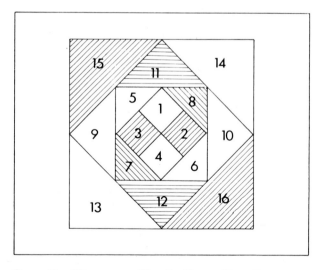

Opposite: **Throw quilt – Indiana Puzzle.**
Machine-pieced in polyester cotton, the blocks are alternated with plain squares of fabric which were hand-quilted (Alison Martin).

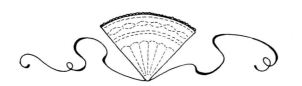

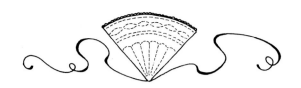

Instructions for Indiana puzzle

Join 1 to 2 and 3 to 4, then join to form a square. Add 5 and 6 to opposite sides, then 7 and 8 to form a larger square. Continue with 9 and 10, then 11 and 12. Finally 13 and 14 and 15 and 16 to form the final 10in (25.5cm) square. These pieced squares are joined with alternate 10in (25.5cm) squares of plain fabrics to form the whole quilt. The whole is surrounded by a 2in (5cm) dark border, a 3in (7.5cm) light border and finally a dark bias edging.

Quilting

The pieced blocks are worked in outline quilting to define the pattern.

The plain blocks have a similar pattern quilted to accentuate the triangular pieces of the pieced blocks. The border is quilted in a diamond pattern. Hand-quilting with mercerised cotton, worked in a hoop.

1) Outline of contour quilting.

2) Contour quilting, curved seams.

3) Contour quilting, curved shapes.

4) Outline quilting on applique.

5) Geometrical quilted fillings.

6) All-over geometrical quilting pattern.

7) All-over random quilting pattern.

8) Traditional quilting templates.

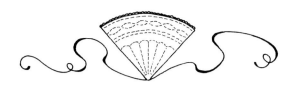

Hand-quilting

Using a hoop

Unless you are quilting a small item it is better to use either a frame or a hoop. A large quilt hoop is more manageable than a frame and just as effective. It is important to keep the three layers evenly stretched. When setting up, therefore, make sure that the backing is smooth and flat. Rest the top of the hoop on the edge of a table so that both hands can be free to work.

Thread

Use a strong single-twisted cotton thread which is especially manufactured for quilting. Match the colour to the background, or use the same neutral colour all over.

Quilting stitch

The quilting stitch is a small running-stitch, evenly spaced; it should look identical back and front. The stitches are much less obvious on patterned fabric. Always use a fairly short length of thread – about 16in (40cm) – and run it through beeswax. Knot the end you cut, to prevent twisting.

To start, thread the needle and come up through the back, pulling the knot through the backing fabric so that it is held within the wadding. Push the needle through from the top with a thimble worn on the middle finger of the sewing hand, and keep the other hand beneath the work so that when the needle comes through it can be guided back up again. Make sure that each stitch goes through all the layers. On the sewing hand keep the thumb pressed down on the fabric just ahead of the stitching. Keep the layers of fabric in the hoop a little slack, so that eventually you can take up several stitches at once.

To finish off, tie a knot in the thread close to the last stitch, take the thread through to the back and give a quick tug to pull the knot into the wadding. Bring the thread up to the top and cut close.

Below: **Cot quilt.** *Made in cottons, machine-pieced and hand-quilted. Overall size 48in × 28in (122cm × 71cm). The 'Star Square' block in the centre is 19in (48cm) square, and is a nine-patch block pieced as overleaf (Alison Wood).*

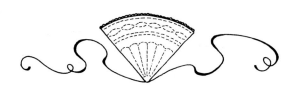

Star square block

Join each row together, and then sew the three strips together. Stitch four rows of border strips around the main block.

Panel star block

The end panel consists of a star block, shown below, at each end of a wide strip

Three strips are then attached to the inner edge, and the whole stitched to the centre piece. Edged with a pattern strip, bound with another strip.

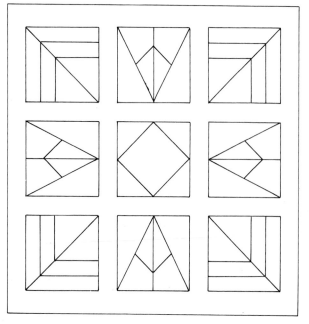

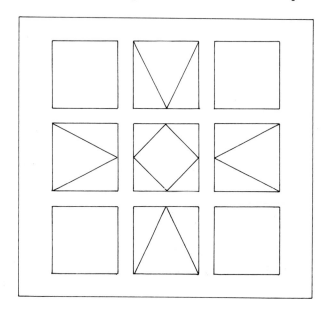

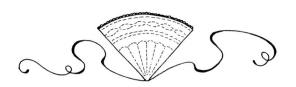

Quilting

Quilted by hand in a feather pattern round the centre area. The central diamond is quilted in diagonal checks, and the offset diamonds are in diagonal lines. The rest is outline quilted ¼in (6mm) from the seams.

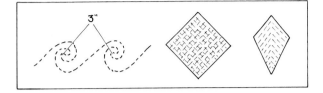

Throw quilt – Double Irish chain (below)

Worked by machine in cottons. Two blocks are used for this pattern:

Block 1 consists of 2in (5cm) squares joined in five rows of five.

Block 2 consists of a 10in (25.5cm) square with a 2in (5cm) square appliqued in each corner. The two blocks are joined alternately to form the overall pattern – three blocks by five blocks. The joined blocks were surrounded by a 2in (5cm) border, then a 7in (17.5cm) white border and then another 2in (5cm) border. (*Alison Martin*)

Quilting

Worked by hand in a hoop, the pattern in the white areas of the main body of the quilt is an original design. The broad white border is quilted with a traditional 'plait' design with a background of 1cm squares. The design was marked on round a template with a sharp pencil.

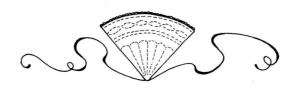

Machine-quilting

Work to be quilted by machine needs to be tacked just as thoroughly as that prepared for hand-quilting.

Machine-quilting is quicker than hand-quilting, but it is not an easier alternative. The quilting has a harder line, while the effect is flatter and less sympathetic to traditional patchwork. For this reason machine-quilting is sometimes better if hidden in the seams – this produces a mirror image on the back and is known as 'sink stitching' or stitching 'in the ditch'. When working this, press the fabric well and open the seam as much as possible to allow the needle to pass through the centre.

Wadding

Thinner wadding is required for machine-quilting, which is not suited to the springy synthetic types. Use cotton or woollen domette or cotton wadding. These all give more weight and a less raised surface which is an advantage for wall-hangings and bed quilts. The disadvantage is that the patchwork will have to be dry-cleaned.

Stitching

It is important when machine-quilting that the layers can be fed easily under the machine foot. Alternate the beginning and end of a quilted line of stitches on each row. Do not finish off with backstitches – take the ends through to the back and finish them off by hand.

Set the regulator for a slightly longer stitch than for general sewing. Use a cotton polyester thread.

Assembly

Start with a fairly small project, for it requires experience to manage large areas of quilted fabric.

It is easier to quilt a large item in quarters or sections and then sew these together. Patchwork blocks can be quilted individually and then joined together in rows in the usual way. If you use this method it is important to allow a little extra wadding and backing, and then trim them to size.

To ensure that the blocks are all the same size before joining them, make a large template the finished size of the block plus a ¼in (6mm) seam allowance on all sides, and trim the blocks to this. When they are joined, trim off the excess wadding in the seam allowance at the back, and lightly press the seams open. At the back, these can be covered with hand-stitched seam binding, or covered all over with a separate backing.

Pressing

If the filling is cotton or woollen domette, flannelette or cotton wadding, the patchwork can be pressed lightly with a warm iron. If any of the patchwork contains polyester fibres, remember that these need a lower heat than cotton.

Synthetic waddings cannot be ironed without losing most of their thickness.

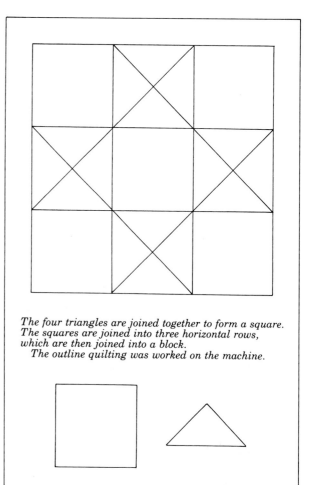

The four triangles are joined together to form a square. The squares are joined into three horizontal rows, which are then joined into a block.
The outline quilting was worked on the machine.

Opposite: **Place mat.** *Made of cotton and machine-pieced, this mat consists of a single block measuring 7½in (19cm) square. It is surrounded by red and cream strips applied as in Log Cabin patchwork (Mary Thomson).*

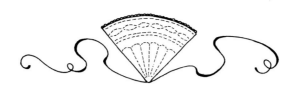

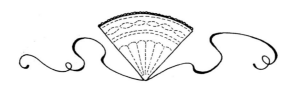

Above: **Machine-quilted wall hanging.** *This quilt was made to an original design block, six of which were arranged as shown in the diagram below left* (Sybil Lewis).

The block uses the following templates:
One 4in (10cm) square
One 2in (5cm) square
One 2in × 4in (5cm × 10cm) rectangle
One right-angled triangle, 4in (10cm) side.
Arranged as shown in the diagram (*right*). The dotted lines show a simple method of piecing.

half of 2	1	2	half of 1
half of 1	2	1	half of 2

Quilting

This was all done by machine – the dark areas were quilted along the seams, and the rows of quilting in the lighter areas were marked beforehand with a water-soluble marker.

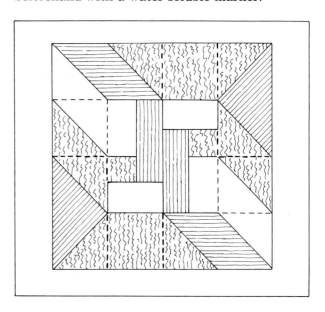

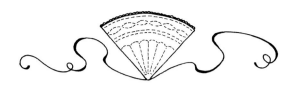

Knotting or tufting

Where any wadding is used, the three layers must be kept securely together. Knotting or tufting is a quick and effective alternative to quilting.

Use a non-synthetic thick thread that will hold a knot – heavy crochet cotton is ideal. Do not use wool because it becomes matted with use. Make a reef knot through the three layers every 6in (15cm). Work in lines, or use the pattern of the patchwork as a guide. Trim the ends of the knots to about ¾in (15mm). They can either be left on top or taken through to the back.

a reef knot

Shoulder bag with reversed fabrics and fringing *shown on following page*

The bag is 10in (25cm) square with a 36in (1m) strap. It is made from a shot denim-type fabric using the right and wrong sides of the fabric. The block is 'Hole in the Barn', and is machine-pieced. It has an unusual finish in that ½in (12mm) strips of the same fabric are inserted into the seams and frayed back to the sewing line. (*Pamela Watts*)

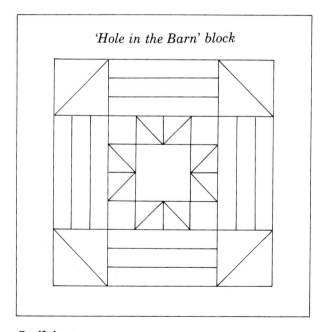

'Hole in the Barn' block

Quilting

The inner star block is hand-quilted in the hand, the design being transferred with a water-soluble marking pen. The outer fringed area is machine-quilted.

The bag is constructed with a piped gusset.

Cream calico bag with knitted fabric *shown on page 109*

This bag is 12in (30cm) square with a 36in (1m) shoulder strap. It is made from calico, and the textured pieces are knitted from strips of calico. The block is 'Variable Star' and the shaded areas show the knitted pieces. (*Pamela Watts*)

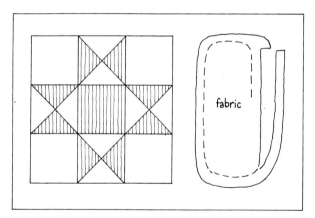

fabric

Knitted areas

Cut a continuous strip ¼in (6mm) wide as shown in the diagram above – it can be cut as you work, which saves rolling it up in a ball.

Knit a test square in garter stitch, then knit the required number of template shapes making sure you include the ¼in (6mm) seam allowance.

Making up

The block is machine-pieced. The gusset and strap is knitted in one piece, and then machined in place.

Quilting

The design was marked out by water-soluble marker.

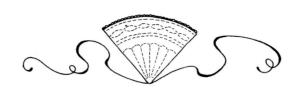

Below and opposite: **Unusual uses of block patterns for bags.** *Below, with reversed fabrics and fringing. Opposite, with knitted fabric. See page 107.*

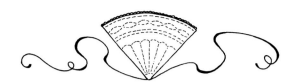

Finishing the edges

A self-binding

This is the quickest and neatest way of finishing the edges around a patchwork.

Trim the top fabric and wadding, and measure to check that the patchwork is properly squared. Bring the backing fabric over to the front with a ¼in (6mm) hem under the raw edge and pin into position. Hand-sew, using a small running stitch around the edge. Hand stitching is easier at this stage than machining, as the fabric can be gradually eased in. Depending on the width, remember to allow enough wadding so that the edging remains padded with the quilt. Alternatively the front edges can be turned to the back.

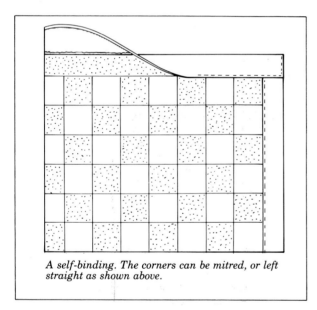

A self-binding. The corners can be mitred, or left straight as shown above.

A separate binding

The advantage of this is that it can be renewed if the edges wear thin. Either use commercial bias binding 1in (25mm) wide, or make your own. Attach in the same sequence as a simple straight cut border (see page 68). Machine-stitch to the right side first, then turn to the back, pin and hand stitch in place.

Hanging a quilt

Originally patchwork quilts were made for beds, but now they are also used to make colourful wall hangings.

The best way to hang them is by attaching a fabric sleeve along the top edge, extending almost the width of the work. Leave a small gap in the centre in case it is to be hung from a centre point as well as from each end.

Make the sleeve about 6in (15cm) wide, so that it can take a variety of rods or wooden poles. Attach the sleeve with a running-stitch about 1¼in (3cm) in from the top edge and side, so that it does not distort the edges once the pole is in position.

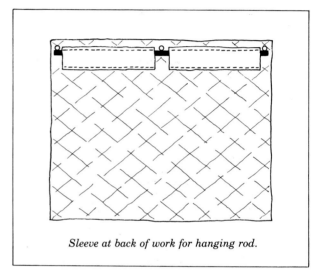

Sleeve at back of work for hanging rod.

Care and cleaning

Make sure that patchwork is never exposed to strong sunlight, as it will fade and the fibres will be weakened. Keep it regularly brushed to remove dirt and dust. Never store it in a plastic bag, which causes mould.

Dry-clean or wash your patchwork, depending on the type of fabric and filling. If it is to be dry-cleaned, choose a specialised cleaners where it will be treated individually.

If all the fabrics and the wadding are washable, then it can be laundered. Wash by hand in the bath, using warm water and a mild detergent – but make certain that the detergent is properly dissolved. Do not rub, just agitate gently and then let it soak for a few minutes. Repeat with fresh water and detergent if the patchwork is heavily soiled. Rinse well, until the water runs clear.

Never twist or wring a quilted patchwork because it will easily break the stitches. Gently squeeze out excess water and give it a short spin if it will fit into a spin drier. Try and dry flat on a lawn with a sheet underneath. Avoid direct sunlight.

Never press quilted patchwork with a hot iron, as this will destroy the quilted effect.

Glossary of patchwork techniques

American block patchwork
A block is a square formed of a number of patches, the squares being subsequently joined to form a larger whole.

Applied patchwork
Single patches or groups of patches applied to a background.

Border patchwork
Decorative border pieced around a centre, or applied to a background fabric. Borders can be made of any kind of patchwork.

Borders with other patchwork
Different kinds of patchwork bordering a central motif.

Cathedral window patchwork
Patchwork formed out of folded squares – so-called because the pattern revealed when the squares are joined resembles the tracery of a church window.

Clamshell patchwork
Patches cut in a shell shape i.e. a segment of a circle – laid in rows and joined by hand stitchery on the right side.

Courthouse steps patchwork
A form of Log Cabin patchwork where the centre piece is often rectangular and the strips are added in pairs on alternate sides.

Crazy patchwork
A form of applied patchwork where pieces of fabric of different shapes and textures are fitted together on a background fabric.

Folded stars
See Somerset patchwork.

Lattice strip patchwork
Horizontal and vertical strips of plain fabrics used to enlarge and enhance squares of other kinds of patchwork – usually blocks.

Log Cabin patchwork
Squares of applied patchwork formed by sewing strips of fabric to a background in a predetermined order, working from the centre outwards.

Medallion patchwork
A central piece of decorative fabric – surrounded by one or more different kinds of patchwork.

Mosaic patchwork
The traditional 'English' method of piecing together small patches made of fabric tacked over paper.

Puff patchwork
Square or rectangular bags of fabric stuffed with wadding and sewn together. The back is flat and the front very raised.

Raised patchwork
Double-sided shapes stuffed with wadding are joined to make quilts, or are more firmly stuffed to make three dimensional shapes.

Random patchwork
Geometric shapes of varying sizes fitted together on a backing fabric.

Seminole patchwork
A form of strip patchwork, originating with the Seminole Indians, where the sewn strips are cut and re-arranged to form more elaborate patterns.

Somerset patchwork
Patchwork using squares or strips of fabric, folded to make patterns and applied to a backing fabric. This is also sometimes called Folded stars.

Strip patchwork
Any patchwork using strips of fabric pieced together.

Stuffed patchwork
Any patchwork made of double fabric and stuffed to form a three-dimensional shape.

Suffolk patchwork
Gathered circular patches sewn lightly together where they touch, or strung on cord, or mounted on a backing.

Index

Information

THE EMBROIDERERS' GUILD is for those interested in all types of embroidery. The Guild holds classes, workshops and exhibitions, and has over 100 branches in UK as well as affiliated branches overseas. Facilities at headquarters include a unique collection of historical embroidery and a large reference library. Membership is open to all. Send S.A.E. for details to: The Secretary, The Embroiderers' Guild, Apartment 41A, Hampton Court Palace, East Molesey, Surrey KT8 9AU.

THE QUILTERS' GUILD is for those interested in patchwork and quilting. Facilities provided include a newsletter, workshops, conferences, museum visits and exhibitions, as well as the use of a library and slide index. Membership is open to all. Send S.A.E. for details to: Margaret Petit (Secretary), The Quilters' Guild, 'Clarendon', 56 Wilcot Road, Pewsey, Wiltshire SN9 5EL.